I0815779

Japanese Woodworking Tools

The Complete Guide to Traditional Handmade Tools —How They Are Made and How to Use Them

from the editors of
Carpentry Tools Basics Magazine

TUTTLE Publishing

Tokyo | Rutland, Vermont | Singapore

Contents

CHAPTER 4

Japanese Chisels: The Key to Advanced Carpentry

CHAPTER 5

Other Japanese Woodworking Tools

Notes

※ The names of carpenter's tools vary from region to region, and we have adopted the names that we believe are most popular.

※ There are various theories on how to operate and sharpen carpentry tools, and this book adopts the methods considered appropriate for beginners.

Why We Wrote This Book

It's not surprising that crafting home items such as tables, chairs and bookshelves continues to grow in popularity. Not only does it add a one-of-a-kind treasure to your home decor, but it also provides intellectual stimulation as a creative activity.

A visit to a home improvement store reveals a wide variety of woodworking tools and affordable materials for your projects. Many of these stores now offer workshops where you can learn how to use the tools, making DIY projects and craftsmanship more accessible than ever.

If you've picked up this book, you might be one of the many people considering diving into the world of DIY. While this book serves as a guide for beginners, it goes beyond the basics to suggest using handcrafted carpentry tools made by skilled artisans rather than mass-produced items. We call this approach "Slow DIY."

Planes, saws, hammers, chisels. It's true that handcrafted tools are more expensive than their mass-produced counterparts. But considering their durability and the craftsmanship that goes into them, they're an investment worth making.

Japanese handmade tools are regarded as the best in the world and are thus sought out by dedicated woodworkers and carpenters.

Moreover, handcrafted tools possess a unique charm and exceptional aesthetic appeal. Their functional beauty is a result of years of refinement to meet users' exact-

ing demands. In fact, there's a growing trend of collecting these tools as works of art.

This tradition has produced many renowned craftspeople, such as Chiyozuru Korehide. Carpentry tools have a rich cultural heritage, and holding one in your hands helps conveys the passion and skill of its maker.

Unlike mass-produced tools, handcrafted ones can be tailored to suit your specific needs as you use them, adding extra appeal to these adaptable implements.

That said, handmade tools can be stubborn and challenging to handle, which might seem intimidating for some beginners. It shouldn't be. This book is packed with tips and tricks to address and easily surmount those hurdles. Starting your DIY journey with handcrafted tools helps you develop skills more effectively and improves your craft more quickly. Makes sense, right?

If you are a beginner, all the more reason to start with handmade tools. Embrace these masterful examples of Japanese craftsmanship and enjoy your DIY pursuits as a dialogue between you and the artisans who created them.

—The Editors of *Carpentry Tools Basics* Magazine

©Photo by Mami Sakoda

Toru Uozumi visually checks the degree to which the materials have been heated.

The Resounding Blows and Flying Sparks Capture Your Attention

When we visited Tsunezaburo Corporation, located on the outskirts of Miki City, Hyogo Prefecture, I was greeted by Toru Uozumi in front of a roaring fireplace. Josaburo is a well-known brand of planes, and Mr. Uozumi is a master planer. Uozumi Sakanami is the head of the company, and makes the planer blade (kanedai). On the day of the interview, the main work was forge-tan jointing. The steel and metal are heated to a high temperature in a furnace, and then beaten with a large air hammer to form the shape.

The steel and ingots are then joined together by large air hammers, shaping them. When the hammer is brought down, sparks fly with the sound of the blow, and the air pressure off the metal were powerful.

Uozumi is careful about the heat level of the furnace. If it's too high, the steel crystals collapse, and if it's too low, the steel and metal cannot properly form. The temperature can only be judged by the color of the reddened steel, a test

The temperature in the furnace exceeds 1,800° F (982° C), and in the summer the room temperature is over 105° F (40° C). In addition to energy and physical stamina, a lot of patience is also required.

of experience and ability. The tense work was completed in about four hours. He says that he's tapped out now at the end! It was a serious battle, so it was no surprise. The process today was only the first step in making a plane body. And so, the nerve-wracking and unrelenting work continues.

The Spirit of Blacksmithing Passed Down from Generation to Generation

Toru Uozumi learned the art of plane making from Utaro Kurokawa, who was a swordsmith. Fukuzaburo's successor, Tsunezo (Toru's grandfather), combined traditional methods with modern ones and established a new age method. In 1947, he established Tsunezo Kanna Seisakusho. Toru became the third president, a position he holds to this day, succeeding his father, Akio, who succeeded Tsunezo. In other words, Toru Uozumi is the third generation of Tsunezaburo, but the fourth generation in the family business of planer blacksmithing. Tsunezaburo's planer brand status was established by Toru's generation.

The fact that Josaburo was able to solidify the status of the planer brand in Toru's generation can be attributed to the spirit of craftsmanship passed down from generation to generation. However, Toru did not intend to become a planer in the family business. After graduating from university, he took a job as a salesman for a major machinery manufacturer in Kanagawa Prefecture. However, he left the company at the age of 20 to help his father, Akio, with his work. He then began his training in earnest and was eventually praised as a master craftsman after all.

Struggling with Blade Distortion

We asked Uozumi about the difficulties of planing: The entire process is a series of delicate operations. The biggest problem is distortion. There's subtle distortion whenever heat or force are applied to the metal. It takes a lot of work to correct each and every one of these distortions. Each plane blade has a different character, and the distortion is also very different. It's like a living thing.

The words of Mr. Uozumi, who has been making planes for decades, carried a lot of weight with us.

The temperature is determined by the color of the heated steel, which is why the workshop is kept relatively dark.

Turning Meiji-era iron into a plane.

How Japanese Planes Are Made

Japanese hand-hammered planes follow a complex process. The process of making a plane is involved. It takes about a day to make a plane blade; from there it's sharpened, and then the blade is delivered to the plane stand where it's turned into the final product.

1

Earthy Ores

The base metal is attached to the steel that serves as the cutting edge and supports the steel section. The base metal has the same function as the steel part of the blade. The best material for ingots is wrought iron, which is extremely soft. First, the raw materials for ingots, such as dismantled ship anchors and iron bridges, are heated to 2,375° F (1,300° C) in a coke oven and beaten with an air hammer to stretch them into long sheets. Once the ingot bars are formed, they are allowed to cool naturally to complete the process.

Waste materials from ship anchors and iron bridges from England, which are used to make bullion.

Wrought iron, a precious commodity, is heated to extremely high temperatures in this coke oven.

2

Hammering

The ingot is made into a long plate and heated again in a furnace. The ingot is then shaped with an air hammer, and water is poured over it to cause it to explode. This is because the steel and metal don't bond well enough to cause a steam explosion. When a steam explosion occurs, small pieces of iron oxide are scattered around with a popping sound.

Goggles to cover the eyes and long-sleeved work clothes are essential, even in summer.

3

Forging Ahead

Finally, the first half of the battle is the forge welding stage, where the metal and steel are attached. The first half of the process is the forge welding, in which the metal and steel are attached to each other. The steel is placed on the metal bar. The steel is heated to about 2000° F (1093° C) in a furnace. The metal and steel are then joined by applying a forge between the metal and steel and striking with a hand hammer. After that, a forge is placed between the metal and steel, and the two are joined by striking them with a hand hammer. The joint is then struck with an air hammer to further strengthen the bond between the metal and steel. If the forge welding is not done properly, the planer blade will crack. This work requires the utmost care.

Cut steel is placed on a bar of base metal that turns orange.

The metal and steel are heated in tandem in a furnace.

Once the desired temperature is reached, no film should form. It's removed and coated with forging agent.

4

Die Cutting

Following the forge welding, an air hammer is used to shape the planer blade. The blade of the plane is tapered to become thinner toward the edge, and this is also done at this stage. Once the shape is formed, a die cutter is used to cut only the planer blade from the base metal bar before the residual heat has cooled. The planer blade with an arched head is produced one after another.

The planer body is cut from the steel laminated bar with a cutting machine.

A planer blade cut out by a cutting machine. The residual heat turns it red.

5

Annealing

Steel that has been fired at high temperatures for welding has a distorted crystalline structure. As it is, the cutting edge made of steel is brittle, easily chipped, and has poor wear characteristics, making it completely unusable as a planer blade. To overcome this problem, the blade is heated to about 1,440° F (780° C) in a gas furnace. The rough crystalline structure is then improved by cooling the steel over time. This is an important process for sharpness.

A gas furnace used for annealing. Heating and cooling can be done automatically.

6

Shaping and Hollowing

In this step, the entire plane blade is shaped, the hollow on the back of the blade (called ura-suki) is created, and the cutting edge is formed. Since the annealing process in the previous step softened the steel, the otherwise hard material becomes easier to work with. The sides and head of the plane blade are refined using a grinder to achieve the desired proportions. At this stage, stamps are also used to imprint product names and other markings.

Plane blade after annealing: At this point, the blade lacks a cutting edge and the hollow (ura-suki).

A hollow is created with a grinder on the back of the blade to form the ura-suki.

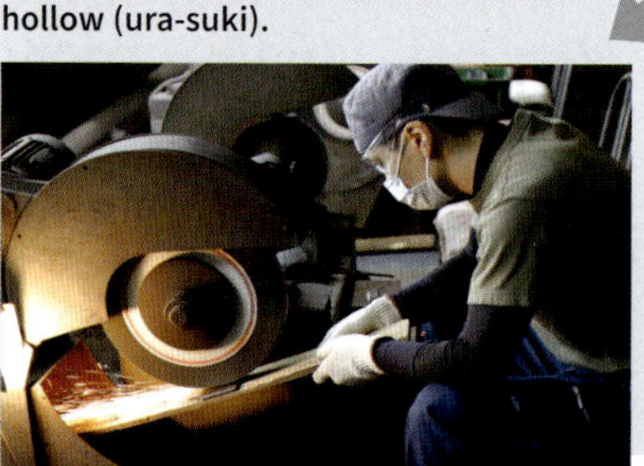

Cutting edge formation: The edge is ground into shape with a grinder—a tense process where precision is critical.

With expert skill, these processes breathe life into the blade, creating a high-quality branded plane.

7

Distortion Correction

Distortion caused by shaping is corrected by carefully hammering the blade. Since the steel and soft iron backing are physically bonded—two materials with entirely different properties—distortion is an unavoidable outcome. Each blade develops unique distortions, and correcting them requires intense focus and patience. Distortion occurs throughout the process, so it must be checked and addressed repeatedly.

Checking distortion: Factory manager Shunichi Nonomura examines a plane blade to identify distortions.

8

Hardening

To restore the steel's hardness after annealing, the blade undergoes a hardening process. It is heated to approximately 1,475° F (800° C) in a furnace and then rapidly cooled by immersion in water. The soft iron backing does not harden, ensuring that only the steel portion undergoes the hardening process—one of the key reasons for using wrought iron as the backing. To ensure uniform cooling, a slurry of grinding powder is applied to the blade before hardening.

9

Tempering

If left hardened, the blade edge becomes brittle and prone to chipping. To address this, the blade is tempered by soaking it in an oil bath heated to 300° F (150° C) for about 20 minutes. This low-temperature tempering stabilizes the steel's crystalline structure, enhancing durability and providing a smooth cutting feel—a vital yet subtle technique. Each workshop has its own secret tempering temperature, which is closely guarded.

A tempering oil bath increases the steel's toughness and ensures a resilient cutting edge.

10

Distortion Adjustment and Back Polishing

Distortions caused by hardening and tempering are corrected again. Using both visual inspection and precision tools, corrections are made with meticulous care. The back of the blade is then polished with a rotating grinding machine wrapped with a cloth abrasive. This removes the black oxide layer from the steel and reveals a shiny silver finish. Though seemingly simple, this is a challenging task. Some workshops choose to skip the polishing step during production.

Polishing: The back of the blade shines silver after buffing, marking the final stages of production.

Final distortion check: Every detail is rigorously inspected for perfection.

11

Back Finishing and Sharpening

The final step involves polishing the back of the blade and sharpening it. At Tsunesaburo, blades are finished to a "90% completion" state before shipping, so customers don't need to start from scratch. This finishing process is the culmination of all preceding steps, where any mistake can be fatal. Consequently, this stage demands intense focus. In some cases, sharpening specialists are brought in for this crucial task.

Back finishing: Mitsuhiro Sakamoto meticulously polishes a blade, ensuring flawless completion.

Sharpened blade: The finished product is now ready for market.

12

Mounting the Blade into the Plane Body

The completed plane blade is sent to a specialized craftsman (daiuchishi), who creates and adjusts the wooden plane body (dai). After fitting the blade to the body, the plane is fully assembled. Once this preparation is complete, the product is ready for market. At Tsunesaburo, hard shirogashi (white oak) is used for the plane body. Like the blades, the plane is prepared to a "90% completion" state, ensuring that customers can use it immediately after purchase.

Products Developed to Meet the Demands of the Times Require Innovation

There seems to be an increasing shortage of successors to the Japanese handmade plane tradition. In the face of changing times and conditions, Tsunezaburo, led by Tetsu Uozumi, stands out. The driving force behind this resilience is their pride in the belief that traditional planes are exceptional.

Expanding Overseas and Working to Develop New Markets

In 1969, there were 37 plane smiths in Miki City, but now only four remain. This decline is largely due to the adoption of prefabrication methods in wooden housing construction, where parts are processed in factories and assembled on-site. There are even carpenters who no longer use planes at all.

The plane blade before finishing work retains a rough appearance. A lot more time is required before it becomes a finished product.

Even with regular cleaning, iron filings accumulate. Their sheer quantity is a badge of honor for a plane smith.

Grinding the back of the blade. Even the slightest overgrinding renders the product unusable.

TSUNEZABURO PRESIDENT TETSU UOZUMI

Born in 1959 to the Uozumi family, which runs the plane-making business Tsunezaburo. After graduating from college, he worked at a major machinery manufacturer in Kanagawa Prefecture before returning to his family business. At the age of 35, he became the president of Tsunezaburo.

Tools that have been used for years, becoming extensions of the artisan's hands, convey the dedication of the craftsman.

Plane-making is often seen as a declining industry. However, Uozumi disagrees. "While the domestic market is shrinking, demand is growing overseas. Over 30% of our sales are exports."

Planes capable of shaving at the micron level are only made in Japan. Confident that these tools would sell abroad, the company has participated in international exhibitions from an early stage. This approach has borne fruit, setting the direction for the industry to follow.

Tsunezaburo has also developed planes for processing laminated wood, which was previously a challenge, and introduced Western-style plane blades. These new initiatives demonstrate flexibility uncommon in this traditionally conservative industry. Uozumi's early career at a major machinery manufacturer gave him insight into the outside world, which has proven to be an advantage.

The company was also a pioneer in direct sales, challenging the previously dominant wholesalers who controlled production volumes. By adopting direct sales, the smiths gained autonomy in manufacturing—a revolutionary change.

Tsunezaburo offers factory tours to the public, aiming to raise awareness of their craft. This is a rare and valuable initiative.

Every May, Miki City hosts the "Kaji Desse!" festival, and Uozumi plays a leading role in promoting this event.

While his approach differs from the traditional artisan mindset, it is supported by pride in creating products of exceptional quality and a determination not to let the plane-making industry fade away.

When asked how he would like these planes to be used, Uozumi shared his thoughts at the end of the interview.

"Japanese planes are the best in the world. If you master sharpening, the plane will meet any demands of the user. Please fully enjoy their versatility."

This interview was a reaffirmation of the excellence of handcrafted planes.

Hote Tsune

The blade uses Hitachi Metals' Blue Paper No. 1 steel, known for its high-precision heat treatment, offering excellent cutting performance. It combines wear resistance with ease of sharpening, making it a highly regarded tool among professionals.

Gojunen

A reproduction of a model created by the first Tsunezaburo in the 1940s, using proprietary forging techniques to remove impurities from the steel. This results in increased toughness and sustained sharpness.

Meigo Ryobo

Made with Hitachi Metals' top-tier special steel, Blue Paper Super, this plane boasts exceptional durability, wear resistance and sharpness. It's versatile, suitable for both hardwood and softwood.

At Tsunezaburo, successors are also being trained for the future. On the right is factory manager Shunichi Nonomura, an expert at plane-making. On the left is Hikaru Sakamoto, a specialist in sharpening and metalwork. Tsunezaburo Co., Ltd. Fukui Yawata Valley 2151, Miki City, Hyogo Prefecture https://www.tsune36.co.jp

Toshitoshi Chiba and Shinobu Shisenobu

The planer stands he makes are known for their minimal deviation. Horiba has been making them for a long time. We asked him about the rewarding aspects of his work and to share any tricks of the trade.

Now Let's Visit Oak Works, the Workshop of Toshinobu Horiba in Miki City

The planer blade is attached to the stand by digging a hole in the stand to hold the planer blade. It shouldn't be attached too tightly or too loosely. When the planing is done in one go, it's fun to work with. However, the size of each plane blade is slightly different, and the planing board also changes irregularly depending on the humidity. Recently, the number of requests from collectors has been increasing. They're more interested in the grain and the shape of the wood than in the ease of use. They don't want to order from carpenters anymore. What makes me most happy is when I hear from users that they're satisfied with their planing boards.

Oak Works, 2-3-16 Otsuka, Miki, Hyogo, Japan.

The chisels, indispensable to the work, are carefully sharpened before each operation.

The planing board is made of white oak that has been dried naturally in the warehouse for three years.

The planer blade is set on the planing board by lightly hitting it with a large mallet.

Horiba's favorite tool used to fine-tune the planing board he's used for many years.

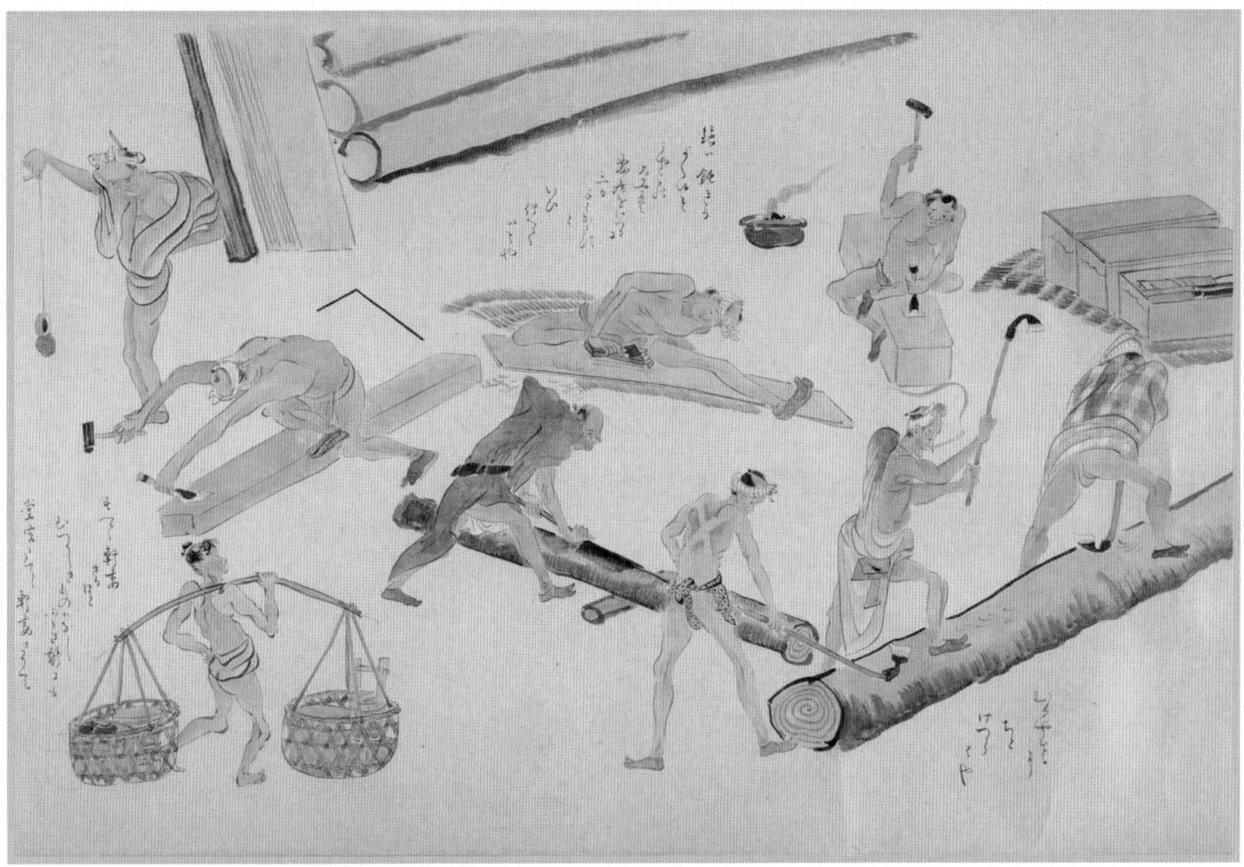

From "Shokunin Zushiekotoba" (Craftsman's Exhausted Words), painted in the latter half of the Edo period (1603–1868). The tools used are almost the same as those used today.
◎Courtesy of Takenaka Carpentry Tools Museum

THE ORIGIN OF A MANUFACTURING POWERHOUSE

How Japanese Hand Tools Have Evolved to Meet the Needs of the World

Japanese-Made Hand Tools

The people we interviewed were unanimous. Japanese carpentry tools are the best in the world. Take, for example, planes. Japanese planes are made of steel and a soft base metal. The steel part is hard to sharpen.

The building is an ingenious way to reduce the area of the building. In contrast, most foreign products are made only of steel. In contrast, most overseas products were made only of steel. This difference in structure is said to be significant. Toru Uozumi of Tsunezaburo explained the difference. He asked, "How do you make a hard all-steel blade easy to sharpen?" The only way is to reduce the hardness by sharpening the blade less. As a result, the cutting ability is reduced.

From the late Edo period "Shokunin Zukushi Ekotoba" (Illustrated Catalogue of Craftsmen), a depiction of kobiki (woodcutters) using large saws for lumber processing.

The Unmatched Precision of Japanese Planes

"Foreign planes lack the precision to perform delicate work on the micron scale, like Japanese planes. They require power for rough shaping but can't achieve fine, detailed work," Uozumi explained.

In short, foreign planes are used primarily for rough cutting, with finishing left to sandpaper. In contrast, Japanese planes can create a finish even smoother than sandpaper. The difference is so stark that they could be considered entirely different tools. This applies not only to planes but also to chisels and saws. Uozumi emphasized that Japan's craftsmanship is among the best in the world.

It's worth noting that the tools featured here—planes, chisels and saws—are handcrafted tools made by artisans, not the mass-produced items commonly sold at hardware stores.

The Simplicity That Encapsulates the Wisdom of Unnamed Craftsmen

Noboru Tsuchida, a well-known figure in the carpentry hand tools world, provided fascinating insights.

Tsuchida, a researcher of legendary craftsmen like Chiyozuru Korehide, has written many books on the subject. He also serves as an appraiser for carpentry hand tools on the TV show "Kaiun! Nandemo Kanteidan" and runs a carpentry tools shop in Sangenjaya, Setagaya Ward, Tokyo.

Tsuchida explained, "Japanese hand tools are simple in structure. Take planes, for instance. While foreign planes use a wedge to secure the blade, Japanese planes hold the blade with a precise balance of pressure in the wooden body."

The wedge system requires less skill from the user, but the Japanese design demands expertise for adjusting and using the blade. It's not a tool that a novice can use effectively without practice. Why, then, didn't Japanese planes adopt the wedge system?

"Simplifying tools makes them less prone to breaking. The rejection of wedges in favor of simplicity may have reflected an implicit understanding that users would develop their skills instead," Tsuchida explained.

This simplicity allows for exceptional versatility. With the right adjustments, a single plane can shave wood thickly or thinly and work equally well with hardwood or softwood. Such adaptability is unmatched by foreign planes. The pursuit of simplicity reflects a philosophy that maximized the tool's potential. Behind this are the collective insights of countless unnamed craftsmen.

The Pursuit of Excellence Gave Rise to Master Craftsmen Like Chiyozuru Korehide

Among the three main traditional carpentry tools—chisels, saws, and planes—chisels and saws were introduced to Japan from China during the Kofun period. However, the saws of that era were small and primarily used for crafting small items.

It wasn't until the 15th century that larger saws for building construction were brought from China. These were two-person saws designed for push-and-pull cutting. Similarly, the plane (dai-kanna) appeared around the 16th century, also originating from China, and was used by pushing it forward to shave wood.

Over time, saws and planes evolved into their current forms, where they are pulled towards the user. This adaptation was influenced by Japan's abundant supply of softwoods like cedar and cypress, unlike overseas regions dominated by hardwoods requiring more force to work with. Notably, this pull-style design is unique to Japan.

During the Edo period, the specialization of hand tools advanced significantly. Chisels, for example, diversified into numerous types. In the Meiji era, innovations like double-edged saws and double-bladed planes with a sub-blade (uragane) were introduced. By the late Edo period, the essential forms of traditional hand tools were already established.

From the Meiji to the early Showa periods, numerous master blacksmiths emerged, among whom Chiyozuru Korehide stands as a legendary figure. Known for crafting chisels, planes, and other tools, his works remain unmatched in terms of quality and craftsmanship. Speaking about Korehide, expert Tsuchida commented:

"His tools were ten times the price of others, yet they required thirty times the effort to make. Consequently, he never became wealthy and lived in poverty throughout his life. Today, any discovered Korehide tool commands an extraordinary price. He remains an enduring source of inspiration and a benchmark for craftsmen."

The section dedicated to Chiyozuru Korehide at the Takenaka Carpentry Tools Museum showcases his handcrafted tools, renowned not only for their outstanding performance but also for their refined elegance.

The museum also features a re-creation of Korehide's blacksmith workshop, originally located in Meguro, Tokyo. It was in this workshop that many of his masterpieces, celebrated for embodying the "beauty of utility," were created.

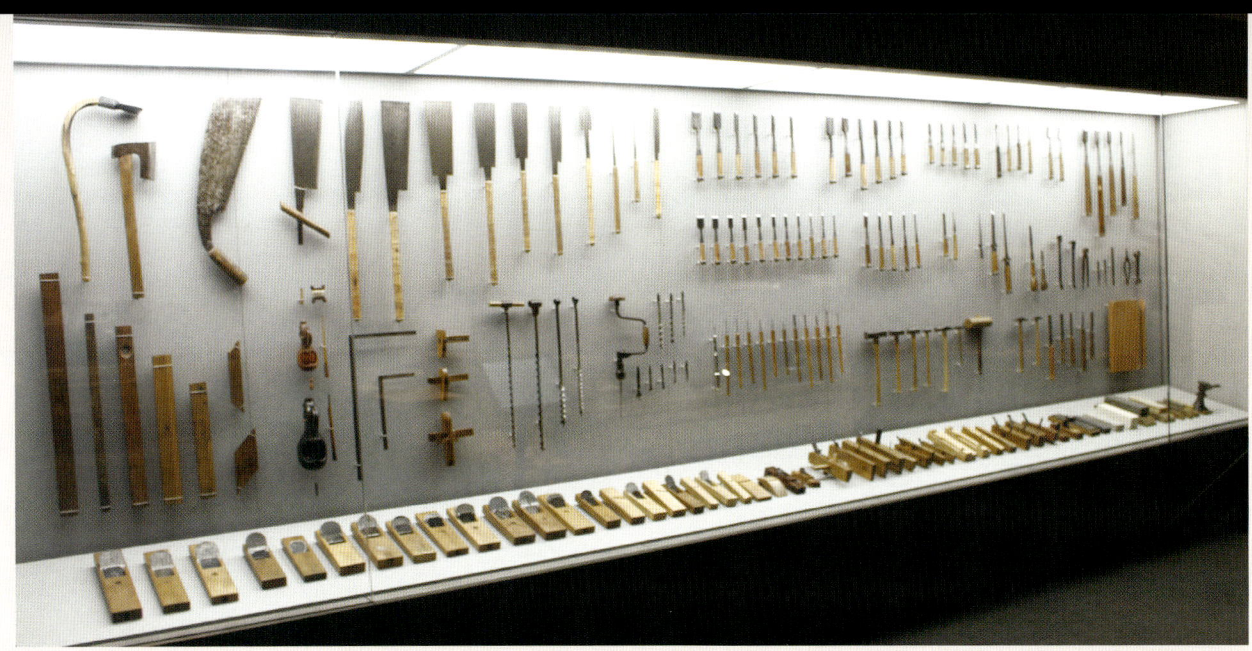

This Takenaka Carpentry Tools Museum exhibit showcases the tools used by carpenters before the war. The variety is astonishing.

The Handmade Tool Industry Is Facing Difficult Times, and There are Concerns About the Continuation of Traditional Skills

There is data from a survey conducted in 1943 (Showa 18) in Tokyo's Ota Ward, targeting carpenters regarding the types and quantities of carpentry tools they owned. According to this survey, a total of 179 hand tools were considered necessary for building authentic wooden structures. It is noted that there were especially many types of chisels and planes. (From *Research on the Work Techniques of Carpenters in Japan*, supervised by Teijiro Muramatsu, 1984). After the war, electric tools became widely used. Additionally, pre-cut construction methods, where materials are processed in factories and then assembled on-site, gradually gained traction. As a result, the number and variety of hand tools owned by carpenters decreased significantly.

This has led to the belief that the pre-war period was the peak of traditional hand tools in carpentry. Nowadays, it is not unusual for carpenters not to use chisels or planes. Moreover, interchangeable blade types of saws, planes, and chisels have appeared, and affordable mass-produced items now flood the market. The handmade tool industry, where artisans make each tool individually, has been hit particularly hard. The industry now stands at a significant crossroads, with increasing cases of craftsmen leaving the trade or closing down due to declining sales, sparking concerns about the continuity of these skills.

The culture of handmade tools, painstakingly built over a long history, is the foundation of craftsmanship. Its decline would be a substantial loss for Japan. However, there is good news as well. One positive development is the growth in exports. To further stimulate this trend, the government should take more proactive measures rather than leaving it entirely to workshops.

The increase in collectors has also become a favorable wind for the industry. These collectors view handmade tools as cultural artifacts and collect them accordingly. This trend can be considered a positive one for the industry.In line with this movement, online auction sites are also becoming more active.

The handmade tool industry also looks to the recent DIY boom with optimism. In reality, the price difference between handmade and mass-produced tools is not as large as one might expect. While some items are indeed expensive, there are surprisingly many that can be bought with a small financial stretch. If you're starting with DIY, I encourage you to begin with handmade tools—you're unlikely to regret it.

HANDMADE JAPANESE PLANES: A CARPENTER'S BEST FRIEND

The plane is the pinnacle of a carpenter's hand tools. A key feature of Japanese planes is their ability to shave at the micron level, making them highly prized implements. But they're also one of the most demanding tools for the user. Once you can produce beautiful shavings, you're the real thing: a skilled DIY planer and enthusiast.

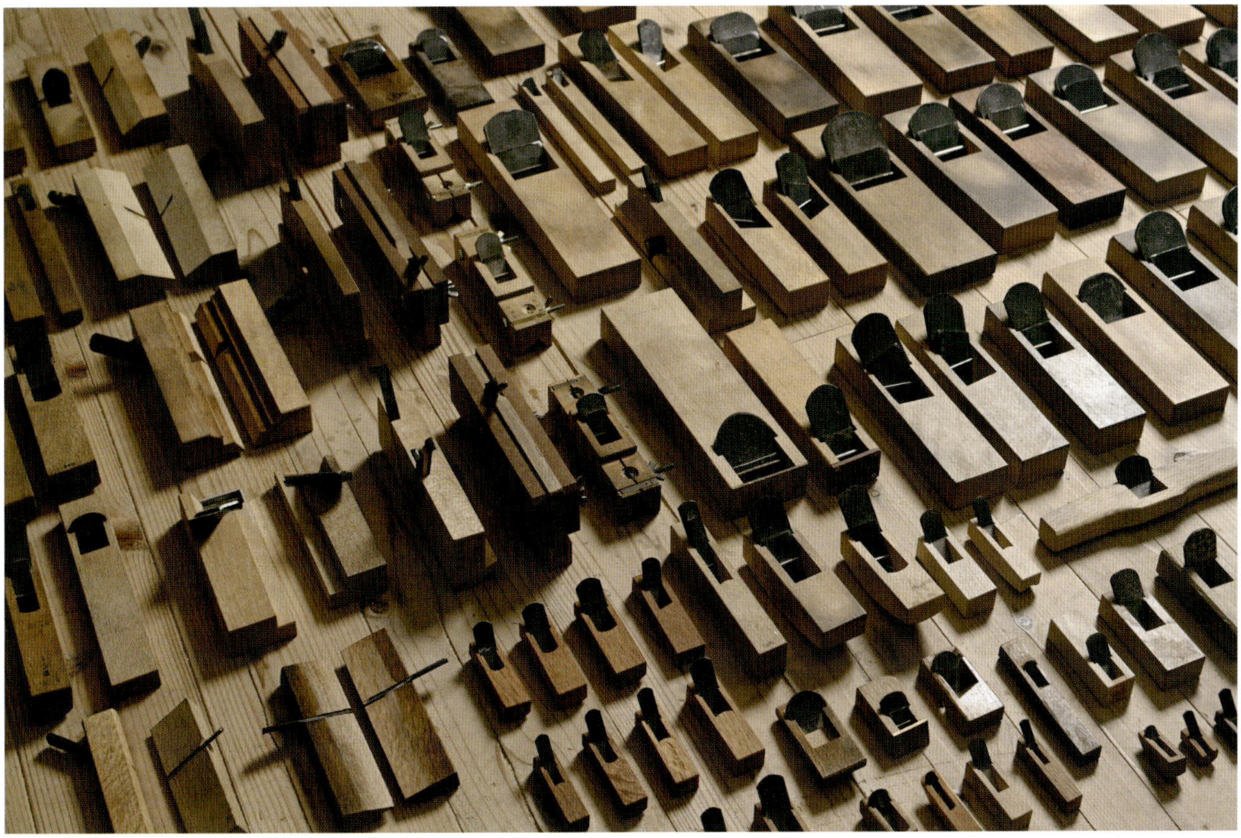

Master the basics and aim for micron-level thinning!

INTRODUCTION TO PLANING

Extremely High-Precision Cutting Is Possible

Careful preparation is required before you starting using these implements, perhaps the most difficult hand tool to master for DIY beginners. However, once you get the hang of it, there's no going back: its performance is undoubtedly the best in the world.

Reaching Peak Perfection with Unique Technology

The record for the smallest planed shaving is 2 microns (0.002 mm) thick, which is an astonishing record. A human hair is about 1 micron in width. Some Western planes scrape off the surface of the wood by brute force. The planer is a very difficult technique to imitate. However, such delicate work is rarely required of Western-made planes, which have been used only for hardwood. The Japanese planer is also the only one that pulls the plane toward the front. The push style is more suitable for cutting hardwoods, while the softwoods are more suitable for pulling motions.

The reason why Japan chose to use the pulling method is that it allows for higher processing accuracy. The technology to achieve micron-level thinning has rapidly advanced. Blacksmiths met the evolving demands of their carpenter customers. It's no wonder that the technology is so highly regarded overseas and exports are growing. The technique of forge welding hard steel and soft wrought iron into a single piece is the most important factor in achieving precision cutting.

A few-microns-thick shaving on display at the Takenaka Carpentry Tools Museum. The other side appears transparent.

The Superiority of Hand-Hammered Planes

There are three groups of planes on the market. The inexpensive mass-market planes sold at home centers have a blade that is not handmade by blacksmiths. The mass-market products are made at a factory, where the steel and metal are combined into one piece. The blade is then cut and mounted on a planing stand. The blade lacks strength, and durability and abrasion resistance are not considered of high importance. You can still sharpen even after a certain amount of pulling, but many mass-market products lose their sharpness quickly and have to be sharpened, while the planing boards are prone to deviations. The best they can do is chamfering the corners of the wood. This is the assessment of the professionals.

Although the blade-change type can be purchased cheaply, the blade change cycle is surprisingly fast. Also, there are limits as to the type of wood they're used on, not being able to shave hardwood. Naturally, the sharpness of the blade is not as good as that of hand-hammered blades.

For your own home projects, you should choose a hand plane, even if the initial investment is high.

While commercially produced planer blades are made only of steel, Japanese planer blades are made of soft wrought iron and steel heated together in a furnace. Here the unique, original technique is practiced at Josaburo.

A Simple Three-Part Planer

There are various types of planes, but the most frequently used and most popular is the flat plane shown in the photo below. DIYers will probably start with this one. The planer blade and back metal are used to shave the surface of the part. A planer is composed of these three parts. The basic structure of other types of planers is almost the same.

As you can see, it's a simple mechanism. The planer blade is not directly fixed with a wedge, as is the case with planers made elsewhere. The blade is tapered so that the side width becomes thinner from the head to the tip of the blade, and is held in place by a groove. This system enables subtle adjustment of the width of the blade. It can be used in a wide range of ways, such as digging deeper or sharpening shallower, depending on the way it's tailored.

The system can be used in a wide range of ways, such as deep or shallow cutting, depending on the way it is tailored. The back of the blade, where the name will be engraved, should be set facing this way.

Planer Parts

Planer Stand, Back Side

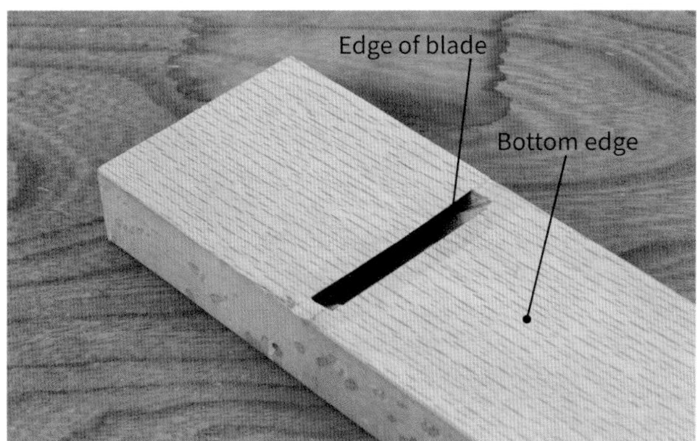

Planing Board Table

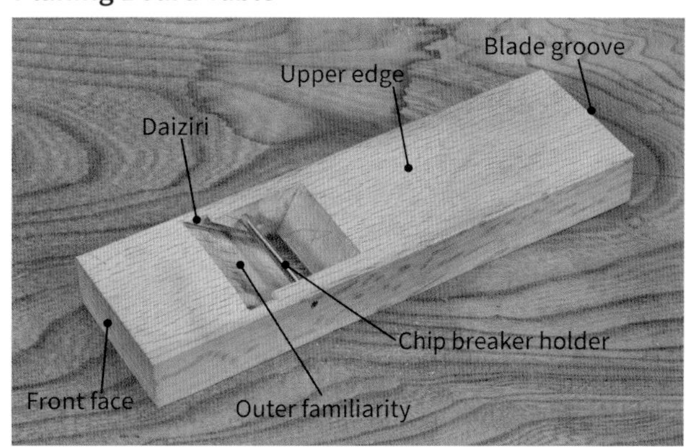

Plane Blade Body

Blade, Back Side

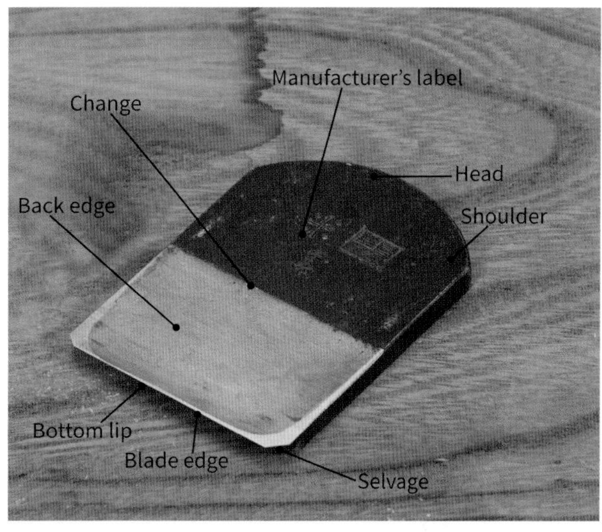

Backing

Backing, Front Side

※The "front" and "back" designations for planer blades were not originally intended to be formalized, but since they're commonly used in teaching materials and in classes, they're used here as well.

From left to right: standard flat plane (hirakanna), long-bodied plane (naga-dai kanna), small plane (koganna) and miniature plane (mamekanna).

From Long Planes to Miniature Planes: The Wide Range of Kanna Variations

Even within the same category of flat planes (hirakanna), there is a remarkable variety based on blade width and the length of the wooden plane body (kannadai). Planes with the same blade width as standard flat planes but with a longer body are called naga-dai kanna (long-bodied planes). While the standard kannadai is just under 11.8 inches (30 cm), this type measures around 15.7 inches (40 cm). The longer body of the naga-dai kanna provides the advantage of achieving straighter shavings. However, it is more prone to warping and requires more careful setup than a standard flat plane. Additionally, the longer body makes it less maneuverable.

This tool is favored by professionals, such as carpenters involved in sukiya-style architecture or temple and shrine construction, and may feel distant to DIY enthusiasts.

On the other hand, miniature planes, almost like tiny toys, are also available for purchase. Some have a body length of less than 2 inches (5 cm), yet they are fully functional planes known collectively as mamekanna (bean planes). These are used for intricate work, such as furniture detailing. They are inexpensive, making them a worthwhile addition to any toolbox.

Best Choice for Beginners: Sunroku or Sunpachi Flat Planes

Flat planes are classified by blade width (refer to the photo description on the left page). The lineup table on the left page is based on data published by Tsunesaburo.

Blades under 1.9 inches (48 mm) wide are classified as small planes (koganna), 2–3.15 inches (50–80 mm) as flat planes (hirakanna), and those over 3.5 inches (90 mm) as large planes (ooganna). However, these classifications can vary depending on the source.

Small planes are used for tasks like cham-

A mamekanna with an overall length of approximately 2.75 inches (7 cm) is particularly handy for tasks like finishing the backs of chair frames in furniture making.

Plane Size Specifications

Type	Blade Width	Shaving Width	Traditional Name	Plane Body Length
Small Planes	36 mm	31 mm	2 inches	5 inches and 5 points ~ 7 inches table
	42mm	36 mm	4 inches	5 inches and 5 points ~ 7 inches table
	48 mm	43 mm	6 inches	5 inches and 5 points ~ 7 inches table
Flat Plane	50 mm	44 mm	2 inches	7 inches table
	55 mm	48 mm	3 inches	8 inches table
	60 mm	54 mm	4 inches	9 inches table
	65 mm	57 mm	6 inches	9 inches 5 point table
	70 mm	63 mm	8 inches	9 inches 5 point table
	80 mm	70 mm	2 inches	ruler
Large Plane	105 mm	(Unpublished)	3.5 inches	3 inches table
	120 mm	(Unpublished)	4 inches	4 inches table
	150 mm	(Unpublished)	5 inches	6 inches table
	300 mm	(Unpublished)	1 foot	2 feet 3 inches table

※There may be slight variations in the measurements depending on the maker

fering corners or detailed woodworking and typically have smaller bodies. Conversely, large planes feature wider bodies to accommodate their larger blades.

The names often correspond to the blade width in millimeters, but traditional names are still widely used. For example, the popular "Sun-pachi" is an abbreviation of issun happu (1 sun 8 bu). One sun equals about 1.2 inches (3 cm), and 1 bu equals about 0.12 inches (0.3 cm), so a sun-pachi plane has a blade 2.1 inches (5.4 cm) wide.

This can lead to confusion, as the blade width of flat planes today is slightly larger than the dimensions suggested by traditional names. Despite this, the historical names persist.

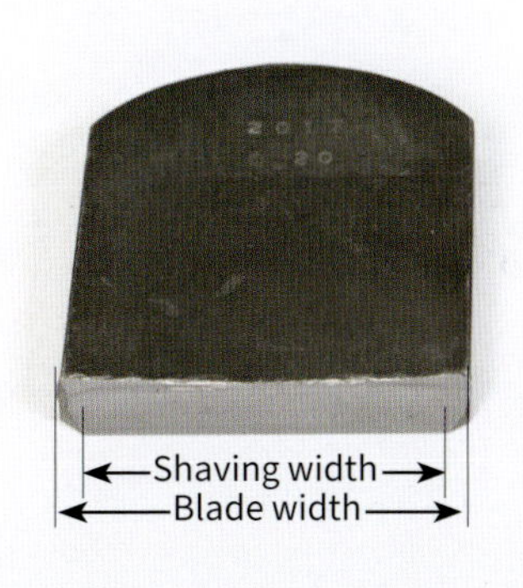

The lineup of flat planes (hirakanna) is classified based on blade width, not shaving width. Accordingly, the length of the plane body also varies.

For beginners, the best options are the standard hirakanna sizes of sunpachi or the slightly easier-to-use sunroku. For women, a smaller sunshi might be ideal.

An expert's eye guides the heating process.

SHAVING MECHANISMS

Technology Incorporated in Hand Planes to Achieve Smooth Planing

Shaving the surface of wood is no easy task. Yet the ingenuity involved in overcoming this challenge and finishing the wood to a mirror-like shine is remarkable. What wisdom did our predecessors use to evolve the hand plane?

Enhancing Performance by Combining Different Materials: Hard Steel and Soft Base Metal

The blade of a hand plane, known as the kanabanmi (planing blade), consists of a two-layer structure forged together: hard steel and soft base metal. The front side of the blade primarily comprises base metal, while the lower half of the back side (marked with the blade's brand) is made of steel.

Although this has been discussed frequently, let's consolidate the information and explore it further. Why go to such lengths when foreign plane blades are made entirely of steel?

One commonly noted advantage is ease of sharpening. The hard, more challenging-to-sharpen steel section is limited in size, making the blade easier to sharpen.

In addition to this benefit, there's another theory: During the manufacturing process, the steel undergoes a hardening process called quenching. However, steel tends to crack during quenching. The soft base metal acts as a safeguard, preventing cracks and allowing for a more advanced hardening process.

The secret lies in the use of wrought iron for the base metal, a material that doesn't harden under heat and rapid cooling. This makes wrought iron an ideal choice for the purpose. Interestingly, wrought iron was originally produced in England during a period of underdeveloped ironworking technology and ceased production in Japan after the mid-Meiji era. As a result, old, discarded railway tracks or ship anchors are now sought after for their material.

In the past, the use of wrought iron was a trade secret within the industry. Craftsmen feared that revealing the use of discarded materials would lead to a reduction in the perceived value of their products.

The chip breaker, set on the back of the plane blade, was invented in the late Meiji era to suppress grain tear-out.

A two-blade plane (left) and a single-blade plane without a chip breaker (right). The single-blade plane is capable of high-precision finishing on end grain and is still used in high-end traditional Japanese architecture today.

The shavings cut by the plane blade are sharply bent by the chip breaker. This action compresses the fibers, breaking their stiffness and preventing the progression of splits.

Wrought iron tends to retain oxygen pores as black specks, called goma. Today, goma is seen as a hallmark of quality in wrought iron, and many people now value it highly—a reflection of changing times. Wrought iron, known for its toughness, also helps absorb the impact that the steel cutting edge endures during planing. Some argue that the base metal plays a critical role in supporting the blade.

Though the origin of the technique of integrating steel with base metal is unknown, we owe a debt of gratitude to the nameless blacksmiths who invented it.

Two-Blade Planes Are Ideal for Grain Tear-Out Suppression

The planes we use today are two-blade planes, which combine a cutting blade and a chip breaker. This design was invented in the latter half of the Meiji era. Before its introduction, single-blade planes without a chip breaker were widely used.

The newly added chip breaker plays a crucial role in preventing grain tear-out during planing. When a plane blade is used against the grain of a board, the blade creates a split in the direction of the grain. If the plane is pulled without intervention, this split causes the wood fibers to lift and tear, leaving the surface rough and uneven. This roughened state is referred to as grain tear-out. Even when planing with the grain, splits can occur. However, these splits follow the grain upward and are trimmed away by the blade, resulting in a smooth surface.

The chip breaker prevents tear-out by compressing and bending the shavings sharply as they are cut. The specially beveled edge of the chip breaker deflects the direction of the shavings while compressing the wood fibers. This process reduces the depth of the split and prevents further tearing, leaving a clean and smooth finish.

Wood with knots often contains mixed grain directions, both with and against the grain. The shift from single-blade to two-blade planes in the late Meiji era was driven by the decline in high-quality timber. Craftsmen began working with wood that included knots and mixed grain, making the chip breaker's tear-out suppression essential.

Despite being replaced as the primary tool by the two-blade plane, the single-blade plane remains in use today for specialized purposes, such as sukiya-style architecture and temple and shrine construction. This is because single-blade planes produce a finer finish than two-blade planes and are also easier to pull, making them ideal for high-end applications.

A two-blade plane prevents tear-out by adjusting the cutting angle, making it easier to handle difficult against-the-grain cuts.

A shallow groove called a urasuki is carved into the back of the plane blade. Surrounding this groove is a thin edge known as the ito-ura.

The Meaning Behind the Shallow Groove on the Back of the Blade Goes Beyond Sharpening

The concave groove on the back of the plane blade is called "urasuki." It is located on the steel portion occupying the lower half of the blade.

Steel is extremely hard and difficult to sharpen, but the urasuki allows you to focus on sharpening just the surrounding "ito-ura."

Without the urasuki, sharpening with a whetstone would likely take much longer. However, it seems that the purpose of the urasuki is not limited to sharpening. In a feature article, Mr. Tetsu Uozumi from Tsunezaburo shared an interesting anecdote during an online interview.

He mentioned that they once tested a plane blade without an urasuki, but the cutting action felt heavy, making it impossible to plane effectively. It seems that the "urasuki" is an essential feature for achieving smooth and effortless planing.

Though my knowledge is limited, I believe this aspect has not been widely discussed in the past. The exact mechanical principles remain unclear, but it is undoubtedly one of the techniques refined through the long history of plane-making craftsmanship.

Finally, I would like to touch on the kanna-dai (plane body). When moving the plane across a board, the kanna-dai serves as an important guide for maintaining a flat surface.

To prevent warping, hard woods such as white oak and red oak have traditionally been used.

There is no doubt that it is a vital part for achieving comfortable and precise planing.

To unlock the full potential of a plane requires effort, time and dedication.

Various types of planes are produced, including one devoted exclusively to carving edges.

JAPANESE PLANES: A HISTORY

The Current Form of Japanese Planes Appeared in the 16th Century and the Japanese Have Used It Ever Since

How to beautifully finish the surface of wood has been a primary focus for carpenters since ancient times. With the introduction of the plane from China, the woodworking process dramatically changed. This key implement also influenced the transformation of a range of architectural styles.

Yarigan-na with a Handle: Characterized by Wave-Like Carving Surface

If you closely examine the pillars of Horyu-ji Temple in Nara, which was built during the Asuka period, you can see that the surface is finished with small, wave-like carved marks.

These marks are the traces left by a tool called yarigan-na, which has a wooden handle with blades shaped like bamboo leaves.

The yarigan-na is used by pulling or pushing, but since it cuts in a scooping motion, it does not create a perfectly flat surface like a plane.

At the time, this was the only tool available to make the wood's surface look neat. It must have been a labor-intensive process to carefully carve each section.

Small versions of this tool were brought to Japan from China before the Kofun period, and in the Asuka period, they were scaled up for use in temple construction.

Though the yarigan-na has been replaced by the modern plane, its characteristic carving marks are still used for decorative purposes, especially on pillars in tea rooms.

The Planes from China Were Evolved with Unique Improvements in Japan

It is believed that the plane, with the cutting blade set into a plane body, which is the precursor of the modern plane, was introduced from China in the 16th century.

Replacing the yarigan-na, the plane became the main tool for carving the surface of wood. This shift was due to the plane's ability to create a beautifully smooth surface, significantly reducing the labor required.

There is also a theory that a type of plane with a fixed blade was used even before the 16th century, but this is not widely accepted.The plane introduced from China was operated by pushing, but over time, the Japanese adapted it to pull in a manner more suited to the country's softer woods. This change reflects Japan's unique approach to craftsmanship.

By the Edo period, the number of types of planes increased rapidly, expanding to meet diverse needs such as carving curves or creating grooves for door thresholds. This functional diversification could be seen as an evolution unique to the Japanese.

Additionally, techniques for adjusting the blade's angle depending on the hardness of the wood or the desired finish became established.

As mentioned on page 29, the dual-blade plane appeared in the late Meiji period. With the dual-blade plane, carpenters, who were technically less skilled, could now use the plane without the problem of grain direction.

In early Showa period surveys, it was found that Japanese carpenters owned around 40 different planes. However, the peak of the plane's popularity was before World War II, and after that, there were no major breakthroughs in its technology. The structure and shape remained the same as in the pre-war period.

Except for mass-produced versions, hand-forged planes made by craftsmen saw a peak during the post-war housing construction boom, but since then, production numbers have declined.

A yarigan-na on display at the Takenaka Carpentry Tools Museum. The blade attached to the end of the handle is used to carve the wood's surface in a scooping motion.

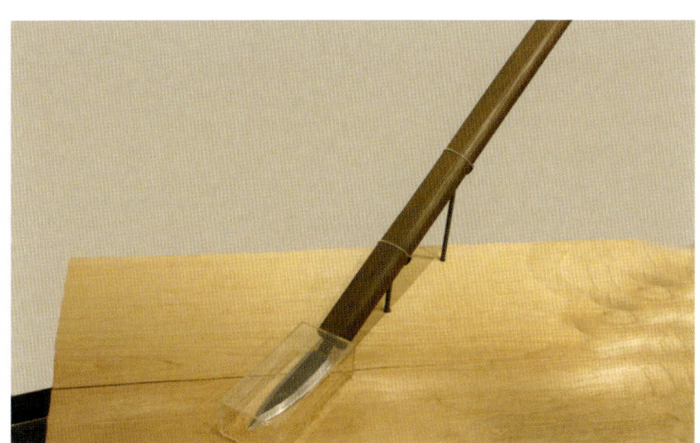

Another yarigan-na display at the Takenaka Carpentry Tools Museum. It was used from the Asuka period through the 16th century as the only tool for carving wood surfaces.

A Chinese plane: it's pushed forward to carve, with handles on both sides.

Various types of specialized planes have been created to suit different cutting purposes.

JAPANESE PLANE VARIATIONS

Specialized Planes Have Been Developed to Accommodate a Variety of Surfaces

The base of the plane may be concave or, conversely, protrude outward. Some planes even have multiple blades embedded in a single tool. For those who love traditional carpentry tools, the world of specialized planes is irresistible.

Planes of Unparalleled Variety and Unique Forms Found Nowhere Else in the World

In contrast to the standard flat plane, there is a unique group of planes with different shapes, collectively known as specialized planes. Specialized planes were created for tasks that flat planes are not well-suited for, such as shaping curved surfaces or chamfering grooves. By focusing on specific targets and tailoring them for particular uses, each has developed a unique shape.

This magazine showcases some of the most notable types, which are likely unfamiliar to DIY beginners. Reading the descriptions should help you understand their unusual styles. That said, the variety of specialized planes extends far beyond this selection. The vast diversity of specialized planes is something unique to Japan. It's believed that the meticulous desire for more precise finishes and the dedication to reveal beautiful wood grain have driven the continuous creation of new specialized planes.

However, while these planes may be familiar to carpenters working on tea houses or traditional temple and shrine architecture, they are becoming less common for carpenters who focus on regular residential buildings. Especially for DIY and home projects, tools like the nankin-ganna are quite useful in furniture-making and would be worth owning. The issue with specialized planes is the decline in skilled plane-body craftsmen. We are gradually entering an era where woodworkers may need to make their own plane bodies.

KIWA KANNA

A specialized plane that can shave right into the corners of an L-shaped corner, available as a pair with left-handed and right-handed versions

The inner corner of an L-shaped area cannot be shaved with a flat plane. This is because the blade of a flat plane is positioned in the center of the body, causing the plane's base to obstruct the blade from reaching the edge. To address this issue, the kiwa kanna was developed. Its blade is set at an angle so that the cutting edge reaches right to the bottom edge of the plane's body. There are two types: one with the blade exposed on the left side and one with the blade exposed on the right side.

In the photo, the one on the left has the blade exposed on the right side, making it left-handed. The one on the right has the blade exposed on the left side, making it right-handed.

DAINAOSHI GANNA

A plane for correcting distortions that develop on the underside of the plane body; a tool worth purchasing for skill enhancement

When distortion occurs on the plane body, the plane blade can no longer remain level, making a clean finish unattainable. The role of the dainaoshi kanna is to adjust such warping in the plane body. It also shaves down the body to reduce friction resistance. If you're serious about DIY woodworking, this is an item worth purchasing. The price is also relatively affordable, with standard types available in the 10,000-yen range.

Since the blade stands almost vertically, it's also called a tateganna or tate-ba-ganna (standing plane or standing blade plane).

CURVED PLANES

A unique form with a curved body, designed to create concave curved surfaces

The two photos in the upper section show the front and back of a curved plane. It is used to carve concave curved surfaces, so the sides of the plane body are significantly curved. A variation of the curved plane is the shihō-sori-ganna (four-way curved plane), shown in the right of the lower-left photo. This plane is used to carve the indentation in wooden chair seats. Both types are prone to wear at the cutting edge, so they are often reinforced with brass plates.

The lower section of the photo compares the curved plane and the four-way curved plane. You can see the difference in the curvature of the surfaces.

NANKING PLANES

By gripping the long handles extending from both sides of the plane blade, this tool is used to process parts with high curvature

It is said to be named after its resemblance to Chinese planes. The Nanking plane handles the cutting of lines and surfaces with high curvature, which is difficult to achieve with a curved plane. It is especially useful in the making of Western furniture, particularly chairs. Various sizes of plane blades are available, and the narrower the blade, the higher the curvature it can handle. With a single-blade plane that lacks a backplate, it can be reversed and pushed in places where grain direction may cause difficulty.

The unique shape of the Nanking plane is particularly useful when crafting the handle of a hammer.

OUTSIDE ROUND PLANES

A specialist for creating concave surfaces with a camembert-like bulge at the lower end

The lower end of the plane body protrudes, giving the body itself a shape like that of a "kamaboko" (a Japanese fish cake). This shape is designed for processing concave curved surfaces, and the blade installed on it is not straight like that of a flat plane but has a convex arc. Due to the arc-shaped form of the blade, there are two types: fukumaru (deep round) and jikumaru (axial round). Also, because the blade is arc-shaped, it is difficult to adjust with a backplate. This type of plane is most commonly used in sukiya architecture.

The blade's edge protrudes in an arc to match the bulge at the lower end.

INSIDE ROUND PLANES

A plane specifically designed for processing convex curves, the opposite of the soto-maru-ganna (outside round plane)

Along with the outside round plane, it belongs to the group of round planes, but it specializes in processing convex curves, in contrast to the outside round plane. It is often used in sukiya architecture, such as when creating round columns from square timber. The lower end is shaped like a U, and the blade itself is arch-shaped, with the center part recessed.

Due to the shape of the blade, it cannot be sharpened on a flat, regular sharpening stone, and a specialized "kamaboko"-shaped sharpening stone must be used.

SIDE-CUTTING PLANES

This plane has a blade installed on the side of the body, used to trim and finish the sides of grooves

Carpenters wanted to finish the often-overlooked sides of grooves beautifully, which led to the creation of this plane. The plane blade is installed so that it protrudes from the side of the body, allowing it to be slid along the inside of the groove for cutting. The lower end is narrower than the upper end, allowing it to be used in narrower grooves. Two types are available: right-handed and left-handed, so both sides of the groove can be trimmed.

Using this plane effectively requires skill in adjusting the blade's protrusion and angle.

FREE-ANGLE CHAMFER PLANES

This is a chamfer plane exclusively designed for 45-degree chamfers, allowing you to preset the chamfer width in advance

Chamfer planes are tools used to shape the edges of square or flat wooden materials. They come in a variety of types tailored to different purposes, ranging from rounding corners to creating subtle step-like edges. The plane in the photo is designed to cut corners at a 45-degree angle. You can adjust the cutting width with a screw, and once the preset width is reached, the mechanism prevents further cutting. It's an exceptionally well-crafted chamfering plane.

A corner chamfering plane designed for shaping edges uniformly.

GROOVE-BOTTOM PLANES

Various types are available for shaping and finishing the bottoms of grooves in rails or tracks

This plane is used to finish the bottom of grooves, such as those in Japanese-style door tracks or recessed areas for fittings. Its design and method of shaving vary by region, as does the way shavings are ejected. The plane in the photo is one variation. Precision and skill are required for long-distance cuts. However, with the advent of rotary power tools, it's less commonly used, even in traditional settings like Sukiya-style and temple architecture.

A two-blade plane with a sub-blade, featuring a chisel-like main blade.

PUSH-CUTTING MITER PLANES

The blade orientation is reversed compared to a standard plane, enabling push-cutting—a highly useful tool

Unlike regular planes, the blade in this tool is mounted in the opposite direction, with the cutting edge visible from the lower end of the plane's front side. When obstacles make it impossible to pull a plane towards you, this tool becomes invaluable, allowing you to push forward to cut. Additionally, its blade reaches into corners. Since a standard throat cannot be constructed in this design, a brass plate is affixed to the plane's front to serve as a substitute.

Various sizes of push-cut miter planes are available, ideal for use in Sukiya architecture.

DUAL-PURPOSE PUSH-CUTTING MITER PLANES

A cost-effective and versatile plane that serves two purposes

This type of plane, called a "dual-purpose plane," combines two functions in one tool. The example in the photo combines the functions of an edge plane and a groove side plane, while also featuring push-cutting capabilities and the ability to cut into corners. This rare tool, unfamiliar even to most carpenters, was handcrafted by a master artisan in Hitachi. The tool comes in left-handed and right-handed versions, which can be used depending on the surface being cut.

The left- and right-handed type of dual-purpose push-cut miter plane.

FIVE-PURPOSE PLANES

A unique plane with a convex-shaped base, enabling five tasks in one tool

This multi-purpose plane performs five functions: standard planing, left and right edge planing, and left and right side planing. Its name, "Gotoku" (five virtues), reflects this versatility. Many carpenters value its convenience and include it in their toolkit. However, adjustments and fine-tuning for each task can be cumbersome, making it somewhat tricky to handle despite its versatility.

A multi-purpose plane beloved by professional craftsmen, capable of performing five tasks with a single tool.

To unlock the full potential of a plane, proper setup work is essential.

PLANER SETUP—PART ONE

Before Starting the Setup Process

We now enter the technical section. A plane cannot be used right out of the box; it requires a series of steps known as its setup. This is why it's considered one of the most demanding tools. Before diving into the setup process, let's begin here.

Start by Checking the Setup Level of Your Plane

Setting the blade into the body and fixing any distortions in the wooden plane body are all part of the setup process. Simply purchasing a plane doesn't mean it's ready to use. This can make the process a bit daunting for DIY beginners.

However, setup is essential to move on to the next step, and embracing this process can add to the enjoyment of DIY projects. The first step is to check how much setup work has already been completed on the plane you've purchased.

Manufacturers often sell planes with varying degrees of pre-completed setup. A plane with 70% of the work done is referred to as 70% prepared, while others may be 80% prepared or 90% prepared. Some planes, marketed as ready-to-use, are fully set up for immediate use, catering to DIY beginners.

However, even "ready-to-use" planes require some setup. Wooden plane bodies can warp due to changes in humidity, and the blade may be set too tightly, necessitating adjustments.

Beginners are advised to avoid planes with unsharpened black steel blades, as sharpening them and completing the setup is significantly more challenging.

Master Blade Insertion and Removal Before Starting the Setup

When you purchase a plane, the first task is to practice removing and reinserting the blade and

Should you use a wooden mallet or a hammer? Each has its pros and cons; the choice ultimately comes to personal preference.

sub-blade. To remove the blade, tap both sides of the plane head alternately. This will cause the blade to rise from the body, making it easy to remove. Be careful not to strike the center of the plane head, as it may crack. Use your index finger to hold the blade steady to prevent it from popping out or falling.

To insert the blade, first push the main blade into the body and tap it lightly. Next, insert the sub-blade and tap it lightly as well. Since this is a preliminary insertion before the full setup, avoid striking too hard, as it may damage the holding grooves of the plane body. Limit your tapping to the top edge of the blade.

Practice inserting and removing the blade repeatedly to get a good feel for the technique.

When it comes to tools for tapping, some prefer wooden mallets, while others favor hammers. Wooden mallet users argue that hammers can cause damage to the plane head, while hammer users insist that they allow for finer adjustments and better control.

Indeed, even light taps with a hammer seem to effectively transfer force to the blade, making delicate adjustments easier. Ultimately, choose the tool that best suits your preferences and style.

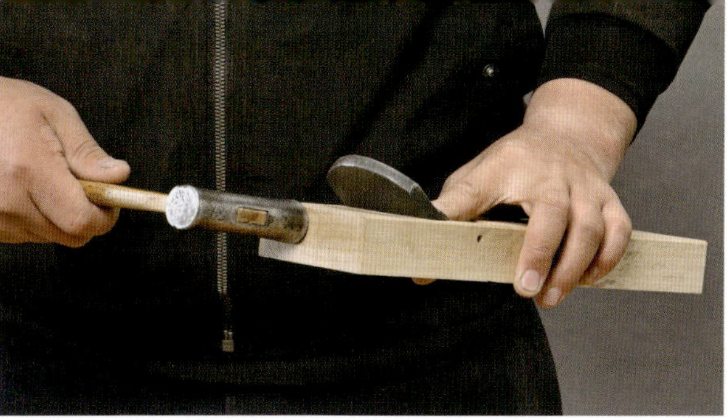

Alternate tapping on both sides of the plane head to remove the blade and sub-blade. Avoid tapping the center of the plane head, as it's prone to cracking due to the blade storage slot.

When removing the blade, use your index finger to hold the sub-blade to prevent the blade from popping out. If the blade falls to the floor, it's likely to become chipped.

You don't need to hit too hard; the wood's natural elasticity helps to easily remove the blade. Mastering the right amount of force is essential.

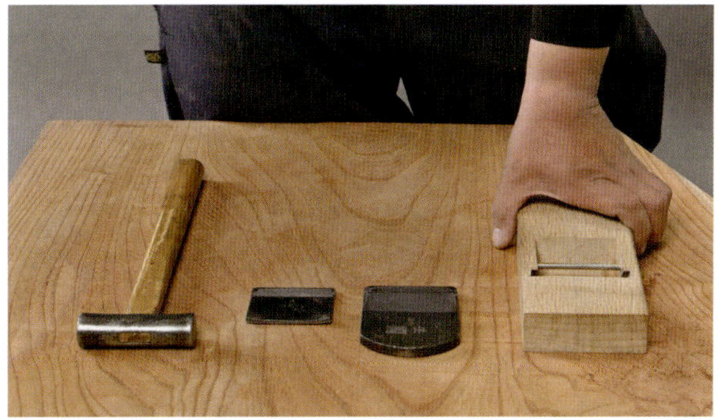

The plane consists of only three parts: the body, the blade and the sub-blade. Once disassembled and laid out, you'll get a full grasp of its simplicity.

Carefully adjust the blade with light taps so it protrudes from the blade mouth.

PLANER SETUP—PART TWO

Adjusting the Blade and the Base: Starting the Setup of a New Kanna

The first step in the setup is fitting the blade to the base. The blade must protrude from the blade mouth located at the bottom end of the base. To achieve this, adjustments to the surface alignment of the base and the clamping groove are necessary. This is a delicate task, so proceed carefully!

One of the Most Tedious Tasks in Carpentry—Beginners Should Not Aim for Perfection

Setting up a kanna is not a simple process. Various related videos are uploaded on social media, showing techniques like widening the blade mouth by shaving it down or cutting the blade's edges with a grinder. Many beginners might feel anxious after watching these and wonder if they can handle such difficult tasks.

Most of the setups shown in these videos are intended for professional carpenters who purchase kanna with minimal pre-preparation.

However, if you buy a kanna labeled as "80% prepared," "90% prepared," or "ready to use," designed to be more beginner-friendly, you don't need to worry. You'll likely be able to skip the complex tasks that may be beyond your skill level.

That said, even if it's labeled as ready to use, some level of setup is still necessary, as mentioned earlier.

The key is not to aim for a perfect score from the beginning. Once you understand the basics, you can make further adjustments later. A somewhat rough setup can still work fine, so approach it with a relaxed mindset.

As seen in social media videos, the methods for setting up a kanna vary greatly from person to person. Gradually find a method that suits you. The setup method described below is a simplified one for beginners. Please note that this is not the only method.

If the back of the blade and the back of the chip breaker don't align perfectly, achieving smooth shavings is nearly impossible. This is a critical point in the setup.

Check the Condition of the Blade and Chip Breaker—The Key Is the Flatness of the Blade's Back Side

Remove the blade and chip breaker from the base and inspect their condition. Check for any warping or twisting. If the product is from a high-quality manufacturer, you can assume there won't be any significant warping or twisting.

If you do find any, it's better to request a replacement, as fixing it can be a complex task beyond a beginner's ability. Next, inspect the back of the blade. The back typically has a shallow concave area called ura-suki, surrounded by a U-shaped flat edge, including the cutting edge. The flatness of this U-shaped edge is crucial for a kanna. For most blades, except completely unsharpened "black blades," professional sharpeners have already flattened this area, a process known as ura-oshi.

Although the precision is generally high, sometimes the sharpening is insufficient, and the flatness of the blade's back is not properly achieved. Check it using the following method:

Color only the U-shaped flat area with a permanent marker, and rub it on a 6000-grit whetstone. The ink will be removed from flat areas, while it will remain on uneven areas.

If the ink remains and the surface is not flat, you will need to perform a proper ura-oshi. For details on this process, refer to page 132 of the sharpening section.

Once you've confirmed the flatness of the blade's back and found no issues, place the blade and chip breaker together.

Align the back of the blade with the back of the chip breaker. Look from the top of the blade and check if light passes through the contact area. If light leaks through, indicating a gap, it means the chip breaker is not flat and needs to be corrected by sharpening.

Proper contact is important because gaps can cause wood shavings to get stuck and reduce cutting efficiency.

Next, place the blade and chip breaker together on a flat surface and press the chip breaker with your fingers to check for wobbling.

If it wobbles, adjust by tapping the ears on either side of the chip breaker's head with a hammer to eliminate the movement.

If the kanna is well-prepared by the manufacturer, these steps may not be necessary. However, some kanna are insufficiently prepared, making it essential to check the condition of both the blade and the chip breaker.

To check the fitting of the blade and the clamping groove where it's housed, apply pencil to both sides of the blade.

To ensure the blade fits comfortably into the clamping groove, carefully shave down the marked areas where the pencil traces appear using a narrow chisel or similar tool.

To Adjust the Clamping Groove and Allow the Blade to Extend From the Mouth, Begin By Checking the Fit Between the Blade and the Groove

Once the blade and cap iron are adjusted, the next step is fitting them into the plane body. Start by inserting only the blade into the plane body and moving it side to side. There should be a little play between the blade and the clamping groove, enough to allow for slight movement. Even with high-quality planes that boast precise craftsmanship, it's important to check the fit between the clamping groove and the contact surface. Plane bodies can expand over time and may require readjustment.

If the groove is too tight, adjust it using this method. Rub a soft pencil along both sides of the blade, insert the blade into the plane body by hand as far as possible, and lightly tap it with a mallet or hammer to push it in a little further.

Be careful not to strike it too hard, as this could crack the clamping groove or the area around the mouth.

Remove the blade, then use a narrow chisel to shave off the pencil marks on the bottom of the clamping groove, gradually widening it. Repeat this process until there is a gap of about 1 millimeter between the blade and the groove.

When checking the blade's fitting, use pencil markings to inspect it. Another method involves using camellia oil.

The pencil marks will remain on the contact points of the blade, so shave only those areas to improve the fit between the blade and the surface alignment.

Adjust the Contact Surface of the Plane Body So That a Light Tap Causes the Blade to Protrude

For fitting the contact surface, apply pencil powder to the front edge of the blade. The process is similar to adjusting the clamping groove: shave off the powdered areas where the blade is making strong contact.

As you repeat this process, the areas where the pencil powder remains will gradually expand, allowing the blade to slide in more deeply with hand pressure alone.

Continue the process until you can insert the blade to about 5 millimeters from the mouth opening using just hand pressure.

You might worry that it feels too loose, but this level of looseness is ideal.

With a well-crafted plane, you should be able to achieve this state after just one or two adjustments.

Finally, it's time to extend the blade through the mouth. Push it in as far as possible by hand, then give it a light tap with a mallet or hammer. The blade should protrude smoothly without resistance. Then, insert the cap iron.

Check whether the blade protrudes parallel to the mouth. If it's angled, adjust it by shaving a bit off the contact surface on the side where the blade protrudes less.

As for the cap iron, if it presses too tightly against the blade, the cutting edge may retract. The correct setup for the cap iron is to adjust it loosely enough that it can be easily pushed in by hand.

Some articles and videos suggest adjusting the retaining bar on the plane body, but often the issue is more complex than a simple bar adjustment. Beginners should avoid making changes without understanding the full context.

Setting up a plane is a challenging task. It is highly recommended to purchase from a store that offers after-sales support and advice on adjustments.

After adjusting the contact surface, insert the blade along with the cap iron and confirm that it moves in and out more smoothly compared to before the adjustment.

Once you can push the blade close to the mouth opening by hand, tap it lightly so the blade tip just protrudes from the mouth.

Press the cap iron in by hand and check its fit. If it doesn't fit well, adjust the angle of the cap iron's side edges by tapping them lightly.

Tap the top of the cap iron gently to push it in deeper, bringing it closer to the blade's cutting edge. Be careful not to let the cap iron protrude beyond the blade edge.

Use a straight edge to check for irregularities in the sole by observing how light leaks through gaps.

PLANER SETUP—PART THREE

Final Adjustment: Flattening the Sole to Correct Warping and Twisting

The final step in tuning a plane is adjusting the sole—also known as flattening the sole. While this task may seem tedious, it's essential for achieving smooth, effortless planing. Completing this process transforms the tool into a reliable hand plane.

A Flat Sole Is the Key to Improving the Sharpness and Performance of the Plane

The plane body expands and contracts due to changes in humidity and temperature. This is an inherent trait of wooden tools.

In fact, the plane can deform even during the time it takes to remove and sharpen the blade, making it a delicate tool.

This expansion and contraction can cause the sole to warp or twist, compromising its flatness. When this happens, the blade won't make proper contact with the wood surface, making it difficult to achieve clean, smooth shavings.

This is where flattening the sole becomes necessary. Let's go over the procedure. Even with planes that claim high-level craftsmanship, the sole can easily become distorted. Therefore, even for a ready-to-use plane, flattening the sole is essential.

When flattening the sole, always set both the blade and the cap iron into the plane body. This is important because inserting the blade causes the contact surface to swell, and that area must be flattened.

To avoid damaging the blade during this process, retract it about 1 millimeter from the mouth. Place a straight edge along each line marked on the upper left page and hold it up to the light to check for gaps and irregularities.

Although specialized straight edges for this task can be expensive, you can initially substitute them with a more affordable straightedge or square.

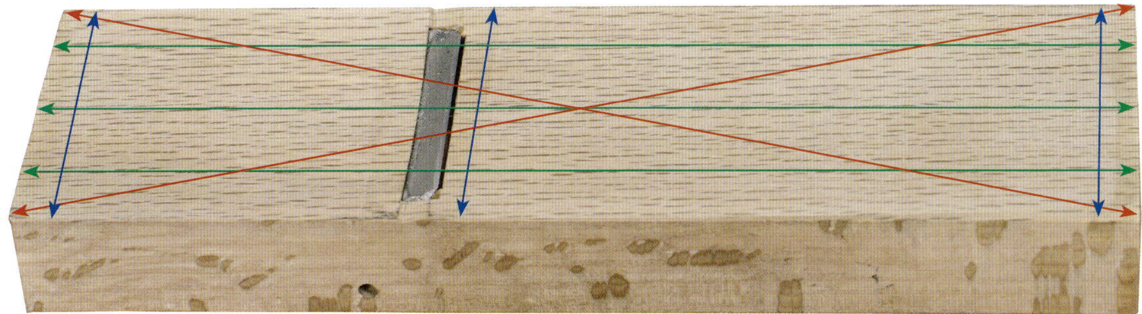

Place the straight edge along the 10 lines on the sole to check for flatness. The most important line to check first is the one just below the mouth.

Once you've identified the warped or twisted areas, use a sole-flattening plane to shave down the bulging sections.

Set the blade of the sole-flattening plane to extend just slightly—only enough to catch your finger. Shave across the grain at a right angle to the length of the sole, aiming to produce fine powder-like shavings.

After each pass, check the flatness with the straight edge, repeating the process until the sole is completely flat.

As an alternative to a sole-flattening plane, you can also use sandpaper for this adjustment.

Prepare a thick glass plate about 5.9 by 11.8 inches (15 by 30 cm) with beveled edges. Glass is ideal due to its high flatness.

Attach 180-grit sandpaper to the glass plate using a removable spray adhesive. Rub the sole against the sandpaper to flatten it.

If you find it difficult to cut with 180 grit, switching to 120 grit might be easier.

While this method is more convenient than using a plane, it has the drawback of leaving sandpaper particles that may adhere to the blade and cause chipping. After finishing, be sure to thoroughly remove any remaining particles from the blade.

You can also find pre-packaged products with glass plates and sandpaper online.

Flattening the sole is a task you will perform regularly in the future, so it's important to master the steps.

The sole-flattening plane is used to scrape away the bulging areas of the sole and flatten it into a smooth, even surface.

Move the sole-flattening plane horizontally across the sole. Set the blade to extend about 0.2 millimeters. If it produces fine powder-like shavings, the adjustment is correct.

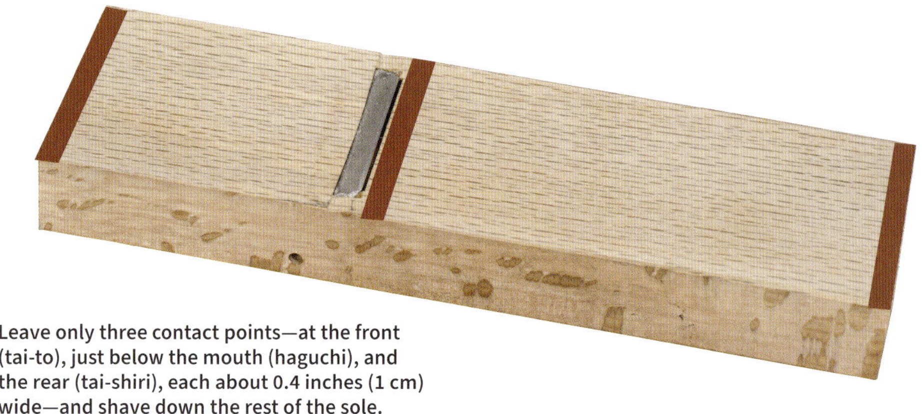

Leave only three contact points—at the front (tai-to), just below the mouth (haguchi), and the rear (tai-shiri), each about 0.4 inches (1 cm) wide—and shave down the rest of the sole.

Slide the sole-flattening plane horizontally to remove about 0.1 millimeters at a time.

Shaving the Sole to Reduce Friction While Planing

Once the sole is flat, proceed to the final step of the setup. Leave three 0.4-inch (1-cm) wide contact points: one at the front of the plane, one just below the mouth and one at the rear, while shaving down the other areas. Why do this? A completely flat sole would cause the plane to stick to the board, increasing friction and making it harder to pull.

Perform this task with both the blade and the cap iron inserted, and retract the blade by about 1 millimeter from the mouth.

As with flattening the sole, use the sole-flattening plane to scrape away the surface, but only remove as much as the thickness of one or two sheets of paper. It's helpful to mark the areas to be left untouched with a pencil before starting.

You can also use the sandpaper method introduced earlier. Narrow the width of the sandpaper attached to the glass plate to make the task easier. As always, if any particles from the sandpaper adhere to the blade, make sure to remove them completely.

Some recommend leaving only two contact points, just below the mouth and at the rear. This method is better suited for thin shavings, but DIY beginners should start with the basic three-point contact setup.

With this, the entire tuning process is complete. Your plane is now ready to use as a fully functional hand tool. Next, it's time to put it to work and start planing.

Proper care ensures proper performance—now go ahead and make the most of your plane!

HOW TO PLANE

The First Step to Becoming a Master: Producing Thin Shavings Across the Full Width of the Blade

Every DIY enthusiast dreams of creating ultra-thin, translucent shavings that reveal the surface underneath. It might seem like a lofty goal, but mastering the basics will make it achievable. Let's begin the lesson on proper planing techniques.

How much the blade protrudes from the mouth determines the quality of the cut.

Set the cap iron about 0.3 millimeters behind the blade.

The Importance of Blade Projection and Cap Iron Adjustment for Smooth Planing

The key to smooth, clean shaving lies in how much the blade protrudes from the mouth and how closely the cap iron is set to the blade edge. Proper adjustment of these elements is essential for achieving those coveted thin shavings.

It's a delicate process, and it's normal to struggle at first. Let's break down the steps.

Insert the blade and cap iron into the plane body. Lightly tap the head of the blade with a mallet to extend it slightly through the mouth. Next, tap the head of the cap iron to position it just shy of the blade edge.

Be careful not to let the cap iron extend beyond the blade edge.

When you tap the cap iron, it may push the blade further out than necessary. Ideally, the blade should protrude about the thickness of a single hair (approximately 0.08 mm). Check the projection from the rear end of the plane, and if it's too far out, tap the left and right sides of the front to retract the blade slightly.

If you retract the blade too much, tap the head of the blade to extend it again.

Simultaneously, adjust the gap between the blade and the cap iron. This is a meticulous process, so take your time and be patient.

For reference, the recommended gap between the blade and cap iron varies depending on the finish:

Check the blade projection from the rear of the plane. Aim for the thickness of a single hair.

If the blade protrudes too much, tap the left and right sides of the front to retract it.

When adjusting the blade, press down on the head of the cap iron with your index finger to prevent it from dropping.

Rough planing: 0.9 mm to 0.5 mm
Intermediate finish: 0.5 mm to 0.3 mm
Fine finish: Less than 0.3 mm
For DIY projects, aim for around 0.3 mm.
That said, it's difficult to achieve exact measurements by eye. These numbers are just guidelines to keep in mind. Even professional carpenters don't measure precisely while working.

Use a piece of wood or lumber with a surface wider than the blade. Test the blade projection and cap iron adjustments by repeatedly planing and fine-tuning. Through trial and error, you will gradually develop a sense for the correct settings. Your days as a beginner are numbered.

Maintain This Posture While Planing! Planing Techniques from a Master Professional

We received expert guidance from Masao Nakajima, the president and master carpenter of Koushou Hitachi Co., Ltd. Nakajima is a specialist in sukiya architecture and temple and shrine construction, making him a true professional.

First, the correct stance. Grip the plane firmly with your dominant hand, and place the middle finger of your opposite hand on the blade, with the ring and pinky fingers resting lightly on the front of the plane.

Align your gaze, chin, elbow and plane in a straight line. Nakajima explains that the key is to bend your dominant arm deeply and lower your elbow.

While maintaining this form, move the plane backward using only your lower body. Keep your shoulders and elbows fixed, and avoid changing the height during the motion.

When planing, the hand on the blade should merely guide it, while all the force comes from the dominant hand. It's crucial to pull the plane smoothly without pressing it down. Regarding blade projection, Nakajima offers this advice:

"If you have strong arm strength, you can project the blade more. Conversely, if you lack strength, retracting the blade slightly makes planing easier."

The dominant hand leads the planing; the other hand only supports.

This suggests that even the ideal blade projection of a hair's width may vary depending on the individual.

Nakajima also points out a common misconception about plane storage:

"While it's often recommended to store the plane vertically, doing so for extended periods increases exposure to airflow, which can warp the plane body. It's better to store it vertically only during short breaks."

Take Nakajima's advice and give it a try!

Avoid this: the posture collapsed during the movement, resulting in crumpled shavings.

Keep the upper body stable and move only the lower body.

Align your gaze, chin, elbow and plane in a straight line for smooth planing.

Why Can't You Plane Smoothly? Common Mistakes and Solutions

Let's explore common issues beginners face and their solutions. One frequent problem is that shavings don't come out across the full width of the blade. Producing full-width shavings is a fundamental skill in planing.

First, check if the blade is tilted as it exits the mouth. If it is, tap the blade to correct it. If it consistently tilts, examine the fit between the plane body and the blade.

Place the plane vertically during breaks to avoid damaging the blade.

Uneven sharpening could also be the cause, leading to asymmetry in the blade edge. Consider refining your sharpening technique. Additionally, warping of the plane body might be the issue, in which case retuning the plane may resolve it. Inconsistent posture while planing can also prevent full-width shavings. Review your planing motion. Another common complaint: "I slightly retracted the blade to reduce shaving thickness, but now it doesn't cut at all." This could indicate improper blade sharpening or issues with the sole adjustment.

Shavings that come out crinkled or curled are also frequent issues. These problems stem from improper adjustment between the blade and the cap iron. If the cap iron is too close to the blade edge, the shavings will crinkle. If the gap is too wide, the shavings will curl. To adjust the cap iron, try planing against the grain. If the board surface becomes rough, the gap between the blade and the cap iron is too wide, and tapping the cap iron closer will solve the issue.

Shavings often clog the mouth of the plane. This might be due to the blade exiting the mouth at an angle or a gap between the blade and cap iron. Retuning the plane should resolve the problem.

When flattening a tabletop, plane only the raised areas.

LEVELING UP

A Training Program to Improve Your Skills—Hone Your Techniques with Tabletop Planing

You've probably gained a fair understanding of the plane by now. However, it's still too early to dive into making projects. First, follow this training method recommended by a professional! Your planing skills will improve dramatically.

Focusing on Thin Shavings Won't Help You Improve—Flat Surfacing Is the Actual Goal of Good Planing

Once you become somewhat able to plane, it's easy to get fixated on producing thin shavings. Since the results are visually satisfying, it's enjoyable. However, thin shaving is just a means, not the goal, says Masao Nakajima of Koushou Hitachi. He suggests that focusing on leveling a tabletop will lead to greater improvement.

So, how do you flatten a surface?

Nakajima recommends obtaining the widest tabletop possible, noting that having knots in the wood can actually make for better practice.

Flattening a tabletop involves planing down any uneven areas to create a smooth, level surface. Start by planing along the grain, then move on to planing perpendicular and diagonally to the grain.

He also recommends practicing by planing not only with the grain but against it as well.

Begin by setting the plane for medium finish with the blade slightly extended, and gradually reduce the blade projection as you proceed.

The key is to focus on shaving down only the raised areas of the surface, like trimming the peaks of hills.

What you shouldn't do is produce long shavings while the surface is still uneven. This often happens when too much pressure is applied, leading to unnecessary cuts.

Nakajima also advises varying the speed of planing and comparing the results to understand the differences.

Tabletop planing offers a wealth of learning opportunities.

Master the Subtle Differences in Planing Feel Across Various Situations

We asked Nakajima about the skills he hopes people will gain through tabletop planing, which is a highly practical exercise.

He first highlighted that planing various areas helps develop muscle memory for the correct pressure and technique, beyond just understanding it intellectually. He also emphasized the importance of understanding how different blade projections affect the surface:

"When the blade is set deeper, the surface tends to get rough. When it's set shallower, planing becomes easier, but you lose the luster of the wood. A deeper blade setting often enhances the wood's natural shine." Even the slightest difference can alter the finish. This demonstrates just how delicate planing can be.

Regarding surface sheen, he explains: "Pulling the plane quickly brings out more shine, while slower movements reduce it. However, pulling too quickly increases the risk of roughing up the grain."

The balance between setting the blade deeply or shallowly, and pulling the plane fast or slow, is crucial, Nakajima stresses. Professionals consider these factors as they plane. It's a delicate trade-off between achieving sheen and avoiding surface roughness. Learn to master this balance through tabletop planing.

Moreover, wood often has both hard and soft areas, which require different approaches to planing. This exercise also teaches you how to adjust your pressure accordingly.

Nakajima advises always running your palm over the surface before and after planing to feel the difference. This helps you verify whether the result matches your intent. Improve your overall planing skills with tabletop practice. Doesn't it make you want to start right away?

Always check how the surface has changed each time before and after planing.

HOW TO SHARPEN A PLANE

The Key to Good Planing Lies in Sharpening—The Final Barrier in Plane Operation!

A plane is a cutting tool, so sharpening it is essential. However, this process is not as simple as it seems, and it can be particularly challenging for DIY beginners. Yet, without mastering sharpening, you can't effectively use a plane. Let's begin by guiding you through the basics of sharpening.

Don't Expect Perfection from the Start—Approach It as a Learning Process

There is a saying in the world of carpentry:

"Three years for hole digging, five years for saws, eight years for marking, and a lifetime for sharpening."

It takes three years to master hole-digging with a chisel, five years to master saws, and eight years of practice to become proficient at marking. But sharpening the plane and chisel is something that takes a lifetime to perfect.

Sharpening is, frankly, difficult. There are many opinions and methods in how-to videos on social media, which reflect the depth of the craft. As such, beginners shouldn't expect to master it overnight. Relax and take a laid-back approach to it.

For a more detailed explanation of sharpening techniques and whetstones, please refer to page 130. The first thing you need to do when sharpening your plane is to focus on back flattening. As mentioned in the setup section, the flatness of the back of the blade is crucial for sharpness, so you need to hone the area around the concave back groove, known as the ito-ura area.

Be careful not to confuse this with uradashi, which involves slightly bending the edge of the blade toward the back when the blade's edge is worn down.

Once the back flattening is complete, you can begin to polish the bevel, paying particular attention to maintaining a straight edge at the tip of the blade.

Beginners often make the mistake of allowing the blade's edge to become uneven or curved. This will prevent the plane from cutting effectively. If you're struggling, there are sharpening guides available for purchase that can help you maintain the proper angle.

When sharpening the bevel side of the blade, you should also polish the ears on both sides of the blade. Round them very slightly to avoid creating a step (called the kanamaki or kanakai) in the material being planed.

However, be sure not to overdo it—lightly pass the blade over the whetstone a few times, and avoid excessive sharpening.

In some cases, you may also need to sharpen the backing metal (uragane). This is rarely necessary, but if the plane's edge has lost its flatness, it's required. The backing metal doesn't actually cut the wood, so use a medium grit whetstone, such as #1000, and don't polish it to a sharp edge like you would with the blade.

The most important aspect of the backing metal is the two-step sharpening process. The angle of the blade's tip is adjusted in this process to reduce tear-out. If tear-out becomes a problem, use the two-step sharpening to fine-tune the angle of the backing metal's edge.

When sharpening the bevel, press the blade firmly with your finger to maintain the correct angle.

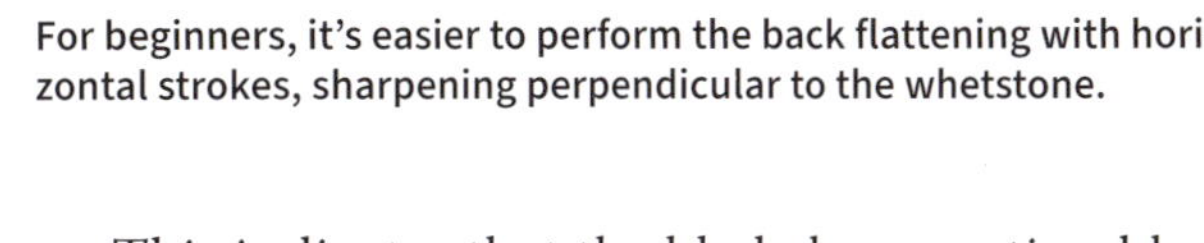

For beginners, it's easier to perform the back flattening with horizontal strokes, sharpening perpendicular to the whetstone.

Know the Signs of When to Sharpen—Learn the Plane's Signals

Some may think that the blade should be sharpened before or after every task. While some professional carpenters do this, as a DIY enthusiast, you don't need to be so meticulous. However, it's important to recognize the signs that sharpening is needed.

"The plane feels heavier than it did before." This usually indicates that the blade has lost its sharpness and has become rounded or damaged. This is the clearest sign that sharpening is needed.

"The surface you're planing has lost its sheen and looks rough."

This is a sign that the blade has small chips. If you examine the blade with a magnifying glass, you'll see the roughness at the edge.

"The edge feels rough when you touch it." This is another important sign. Occasionally, run your fingers over the blade to check its condition.

"The planed surface is scratched, and the shavings are torn."

This indicates that the blade has a noticeable chip. If the chip is barely visible, you can continue working, but if it's more significant, you'll need to do some serious sharpening with a diamond whetstone, which can take quite a bit of time.

These are the main signs that sharpening is needed. However, if you're able to produce thin, full-width shavings, then you can continue working without sharpening.

This principle also applies to plane adjustments—if there's some distortion but you're still able to plane, then there's no need to worry. Sharpening is a delicate process, but it's also flexible. Approach it with a bit of tolerance, and you'll be fine.

Losing the ito-ura around the back groove affects cutting performance.

MAINTENANCE AND STORAGE

Proper Care Is the Key to Maintaining Your Favorite Plane's Performance

A plane is a demanding tool that requires a lot of attention and care. However, if you respond to its needs, it will perform wonderfully. The key is to never neglect its maintenance.

When the Ito-Ura Wears Out, Perform Back Flattening to Restore It

With repeated sharpening, the ito-ura (the back groove) on the blade will gradually wear down. If you continue sharpening, the ito-ura will disappear, and the blade will lose its edge, a condition known as uragire. Once this happens, smooth planing becomes difficult, if not impossible.

Back flattening helps prevent the disappearance of the ito-ura. By gently tapping the bevel of the blade with a hammer (called genno), the edge is bent slightly toward the back, allowing the ito-ura to be restored. This process is delicate, so take great care when tapping the bevel area. Back flattening is also used when, despite pressing the blade against a whetstone, certain areas don't come into contact with the stone, leaving the blade uneven. In these cases, back flattening helps achieve a flat edge.

The back flattening process involves gently tapping the bevel on the anvil to bend the edge toward the back, restoring the ito-ura.

Fine Maintenance Is Essential for Maintaining the Condition of Your Plane

In the past, carpenters were disciplined about the care of their tools. It's said that if a plane was left in direct sunlight or exposed to water, the master carpenter would reprimand the apprentice, as it could distort the plane's body.

Leaving a plane in a windy location or storing it in a damp place can lead to warping or twisting of the body. To avoid this, professional craftsman Masao Nakajima of Takumi Hitachi takes extra care in managing his planes. For instance, he covers his planes with cloth on rainy days to prevent moisture from entering. DIY enthusiasts should take note of these professional habits.

When storing a plane, Nakajima advises not to leave it exposed but to keep it in a cloth plane bag. These bags are affordable and should be purchased alongside the plane.

When storing, it is best not to remove the blade. Instead, retract it just slightly to prevent damage to the edge. However, Nakajima goes a step further and ensures that the blade is extended by the width of a single hair. This helps prevent warping of the plane body. While the blade can be slightly extended when stored in a cloth bag, the edge won't be damaged.

For those aiming for high-level planing, adopting Nakajima's method might be a good idea. Some people recommend an "oil bed," where the plane body is soaked in oil for storage. This method is said to prevent distortion of the plane body. However, Nakajima points out that it's an outdated technique. He explains, "While it was practiced in the past, fewer people recommend using an oil bed today. It can dirty the material you're planing, so I never do it."

As for oiling, Nakajima suggests not applying oil directly to the blade but instead wiping it with an oily cloth. This method is just right for keeping the blade in good condition.

If you want to truly make the plane your own, paying attention to both its maintenance and storage is crucial. This care will allow the tool to perform at its best.

By storing your plane in a cloth bag, you can keep the blade extended without worrying about it getting damaged.

In addition to cloth bags, there are various types of plane bags available on the market, including those made from vinyl leather.

AN INTERVIEW WITH AN EXPERT

If You Want to Improve, Learn to Love Your Tools

The company that assisted with technical guidance and provided support for photographing carpentry hand tools is Koushou Hitachi, based in Tsuchiura City, Ibaraki Prefecture. The owner and master carpenter, Masao Nakajima, took a moment to share his philosophy on tools.

Nakajima's handmade inkpot—reflecting his skill as a sukiya carpenter.

Studied Traditional Japanese Architecture and Temple Construction in Kyoto

Carpentry workshops are often cluttered with tools, usually disorganized. However, Koushou Hitachi's workshop is neat, with meticulous organization. They own over 100 planes, chisels, and saws, and storage is carefully planned for efficiency, considering usage purposes, work sequence, and workflow. The floor is covered with soft cedar wood to prevent damaging the blades if tools are accidentally dropped.

Chisels and other tools are used until the steel parts are completely worn down, and even tools that are no longer needed are creatively repurposed for other uses. This reflects Nakajima's love for his tools and his serious approach to craftsmanship.

Before we discuss Nakajima's views on tools, let's touch on his background. After graduating from university, he couldn't find a job he was passionate about. He returned to his family home in Hitachi-Ota, Ibaraki, and while looking for something to do, he happened to take a part-time job at a local construction company. It was there that he suddenly discovered the joy of carpentry.

"It felt like something clicked," he recalls. He then moved to Kyoto to study at the prestigious Nakamura Soji Construction Company, where he learned sukiya (traditional Japanese tea house) construction and temple architecture at the Kitamura Makoto Construction Company. After finishing his apprenticeship, he established Koushou Hitachi, specializing in sukiya and temple construction.

MASAO NAKAJIMA
CEO AND MASTER CARPENTER OF KOUSHOU HITACHI

After graduating from college, Nakajima pursued carpentry, studying sukiya architecture and temple construction in Kyoto. In 2018, he founded Koushou Hitachi Co., Ltd. in Higashinamiki Town, Tsuchiura City, Ibaraki Prefecture. He is a licensed architect, real estate agent and financial planner. https://kousyou-hitachi.com

The Mountain Gate and Decorative Fence of Muniyakuji Temple, a Nichiren sect temple in Hitachinaka City, built by Koushou Hitachi.

Sharpening Chisels and Planes Continuously Is the First Step to Improvement

Carpentry hand tools must be nurtured and cared for to become usable—this is the view of Nakajima, who has worked closely with tools for many years.

"I believe that when you buy a tool, it's only about 10% complete. It's not made by a professional carpenter; it's made by a blacksmith. The goal is to take it from the blacksmith's version to a fully functional, perfect tool that is 100% ready for use in the field. I'm always thinking about how to bring it to that level." Indeed, planes and chisels require pre-work, like tuning and sharpening, before they are ready for use. However, Nakajima continued, it's not just about that.

"During my apprenticeship in Kyoto, I had the chance to see the hand tools of senior carpenters. At first glance, their tools seemed untouched, but in fact, they had extensively modified them. This really surprised me."

When he asked about it, the senior carpenters explained their reasons. Some of their explanations were questionable, but Nakajima was deeply impressed by their dedication to modifying and adapting their tools, treating them as an extension of their own hands and feet.

Tools are meant to evolve. Nakajima learned this from his mentors.

"If you're satisfied with what you buy, you won't be able to tell if the tool is difficult to use."

The joy of carpentry hand tools, Nakajima says, is in the ability to grow and shape them with your own hands. This is the essence of working with tools.

He also said, "People who love their tools will definitely improve faster." So, how does one become someone who loves tools?

"It all started when I was given a chisel by my master at the first construction company I worked for. He told me to sharpen it every day, so I did, and that's when I really grew attached to it. I ended up loving tools."

A famous master of temple architecture also commands his apprentices to simply keep sharpening tools.

Even DIY beginners should, with an empty mind, sharpen chisels and planes. That is the first step to improvement, according to Nakajima's valuable advice.

Standing at the center of the exhibition hall is a life-sized architectural model of the main hall (Kondō) of Tōshōdaiji Temple.
◎ Photo courtesy of the Takenaka Carpentry Tools Museum.

JAPAN'S ONLY MUSEUM DEDICATED TO HAND TOOLS

The Takanaka Carpentry Tools Museum in Kobe Is a DIY Wonderland

Over 30,000 Carpentry Tools Collected and Curated by Takenaka Corporation, a Major Construction Company

Just a short walk from the central ticket gate of Sanyo Shinkansen's Shin-Kobe Station lies the Takenaka Carpentry Tools Museum, nestled in a forest visible from the train platform.

Passing through a traditional Japanese-style gate, you'll find a sleek glass-paneled single-story building surrounded by trees. This is the museum's main building, with two underground floors dedicated to exhibitions.

The building itself is a point of interest. It features a roof made of lightweight Awaji tiles, walls coated with precious Jūraku clay plaster, and beautifully extended eaves. The lobby's ceiling, resembling the bottom of a ship, is constructed from a combination of cedarwood. Architecture enthusiasts will want to examine every detail.

The museum was established by Takenaka Corporation, a leading construction company. The building showcases the pinnacle of wooden architecture, built by top-tier craftsmen. The Takenaka Carpentry Tools Museum has a history spanning nearly 40 years. It first opened in 1984 in Nakayamate-dōri, Kobe, with the aim of collecting and preserving exceptional carpentry tools and passing down the spirit of master toolsmiths.

The "Bringing Wood to Life" section, located on the second underground floor, allows visitors to learn about the differences in wood properties depending on the tree species.

◎ Photo courtesy of the Takenaka Carpentry Tools Museum.

In 2014, on its 30th anniversary, the museum moved to its current location. To this day, it remains Japan's only full-scale museum dedicated to carpentry tools. Carpentry tools are consumables that are typically discarded after use. Preserving them as cultural heritage is a meaningful endeavor. By appreciating these tools, one can also glimpse the spirit and wisdom of the Japanese people. The museum houses over 30,000 tools, with around 1,000 on display at any given time. It actively hosts special exhibitions and lectures, enthusiastically sharing information with the public.

As Hand Tools Evolved, Construction Methods Changed Dramatically

Descending from the lobby to the underground exhibition hall, you are greeted by a central display: a structural model mounted on a circular pillar. It is a life-size replica of the main hall of Tōshōdaiji Temple, originally built in the Nara period and faithfully recreated by master temple carpenter Mitsuo Ogawa.

The museum building, seen after passing through the entrance gate, is a masterpiece that harmonizes with the surrounding landscape. It incorporates numerous elements of traditional Japanese architecture.

It is astounding that such a complex structure was built during a time when tools like planes and sophisticated saws had not yet been introduced. The skill of ancient carpenters is truly impressive. Now, it's time to explore the museum. There are seven sections in total, but for a comprehensive understanding, it's best to start with the "Journey Through History" section.

From the Jomon period, where only stone axes were used, various hand tools were introduced from China, gradually transforming the methods of wood processing and construction.

The most significant revolution came with the introduction of the saw. In the Muromachi period, the birth of the shoin-zukuri architectural style, the prototype of the traditional Japanese room, was made possible because saws could easily produce thin boards and slender wooden materials. There is much to learn in this section.

In the "Learning from the Master Builders" section, the craftsmanship of carpenters and how they interact with their tools is showcased. The "Tools and Handwork" section delves deeper into the philosophy behind tool use.

On display: the plane blade shinunmu by Chiyozuru Korehide and the hammer yamabiko. These are iconic masterpieces in the world of hand tools.

Tetsunosuke Miyano II, a master sawsmith, is regarded as the pinnacle of his craft. He rejected Western steel and remained committed to producing saws using traditional Japanese tamahagane steel.

TAKENAKA CARPENTRY TOOLS MUSEUM

7-5-1 Kumochi-cho, Chuo-ku, Kobe City, Hyogo Prefecture
• Opening Hours: 9:30 AM–4:30 PM
• Closed: Mondays (or the following day if Monday is a public holiday) and during the New Year holidays
• Access: About a 3-minute walk from the central ticket gate of Shin-Kobe Station on the Sanyo Shinkansen, or from the north exit of Kobe Municipal Subway's Shin-Kobe Station
https://www.dougukan.jp

On the first underground floor, the "Around the World" section introduces hand tools from different countries. Comparing them with Japanese tools highlights the Japanese dedication to precision in woodwork.

Master Craftsmen Devoted Their Entire Being to Breathing Life into Hand Tools

On the second underground floor, there are three exhibition sections. In the "Traditional Japanese Aesthetics" section, a life-size structural model of the tea house at Gyokurin-in, a sub-temple of Daitoku-ji in Kyoto, is on display.

This model, with its exposed structural elements, demonstrates the precision of sukiya carpentry. Witnessing this supreme craftsmanship offers a profound appreciation of the depth of Japanese architecture.

Next is the "Bringing Wood to Life" section, where visitors can learn about the properties of wood based on tree species. An impressive display features 11 different types of wooden pillars. Finally, head to the "Brilliance of Master Craftsmen" section, where you can closely observe works by legendary toolsmiths like Chiyozuru Korehide, Miyano Tetsunosuke II, and Zenzaemon II and III.

These craftsmen never intended to create works of art or leave behind a legacy. They simply dedicated themselves to exceeding their clients' expectations, hammering out each piece in the corners of their workshops with utmost care.

This dedication captivated people and earned them high praise as examples of "functional beauty." You'll leave with a lingering impression of what it means for a tool to possess a soul.

After exploring all seven sections, visitors will appreciate the museum's hands-on exhibits, allowing them to touch and interact with the tools. This is a remarkable way to enhance understanding. Japan's only carpentry tools museum is truly a DIY wonderland.

SUPERB JAPANESE SAWS: THE PERFECT TOOLS FOR CUTTING

Among the three essential carpentry hand tools, the saw is likely the most familiar. Everyone has probably held one at least once. However, because it's seen as a basic if essential cutting tool, it's often taken for granted. Many saws actually incorporate numerous innovations designed specifically for cutting wood. So let's take a new and deeper look at this often underappreciated implement.

Cutting with hand-forged saws while honoring their creator.

SAW SCIENCE: AN INTRODUCTION

Even in the Era of Replaceable Blades, Hand-Forged Saws Crafted by Skilled Blacksmiths Still Outperform

While replaceable-blade saws dominate the market, some critics claim that hand-forged saws are on the verge of extinction. However, the charm of these traditional tools, rooted in history and tradition, remains undiminished.

The Joy of Cutting with Hand-Forged Saws

We now live in an era where replaceable-blade saws are the norm. With a single saw, you can cut vertically, horizontally, or diagonally, even slicing through thick, glue-laminated plywood.

When the blade dulls, you simply swap it out—an easy and affordable solution. Additionally, modern technology allows for the instantaneous hardening of the blade's edge, providing sharp and precise cuts.

Given these advantages, it's no wonder that hand-forged saws struggle to compete. Yet, I recommend hand-forged saws because they offer a unique experience and joy that replaceable-blade saws cannot replicate. Each hand-forged saw represents a culmination of refined techniques passed down through generations.

Craftsmen harness these skills and deliver finely honed tools to their users, making them more than just tools—they are a cultural artifact.

Owning a hand-forged saw means respecting the craftsman's dedication to their craft and engaging in a "conversation" with the maker through the tool. When replaceable-blade saws and music CDs appeared around the same time, many preferred the convenience and high-quality sound of CDs.

If we compare, a hand-forged saw is like an analog record—a classic that deserves revival, much like how vinyl records have regained popularity. Why not add a hand-forged saw to your collection as a different type of tool? You may find yourself growing deeply attached to it.

Craftsmanship of Hand-Forged Saws

Let's delve deeper into the world of hand-forged saws. There are two main types of hand-forged saws: rip saws and crosscut saws. Rip saws cut along the wood grain, while crosscut saws cut perpendicular to the grain.

In the Meiji era, double-edged saws that combined both rip and crosscut functions became popular and remain the standard today. Saws are made from steel plates, with teeth carved into them. As you may know, Japanese saws cut on the pull stroke, which is the opposite of Western saws that cut on the push stroke. Although the saw is made from a single steel plate, its thickness is not uniform.

The base (near the handle) is thicker, while the tip is thinner. This variation in thickness prevents the saw blade from deforming during use. During cutting, the blade's edge heats up the most, creating a temperature difference between the edge and the center of the blade.

This temperature difference causes the blade to expand at different rates, leading to warping.

To counteract this, the central part of the saw blade is thinned, allowing it to absorb the expansion caused by heat. Such mechanical considerations are what make hand-forged saws efficient and comfortable to use.

Parts of a Double-Edged Saw

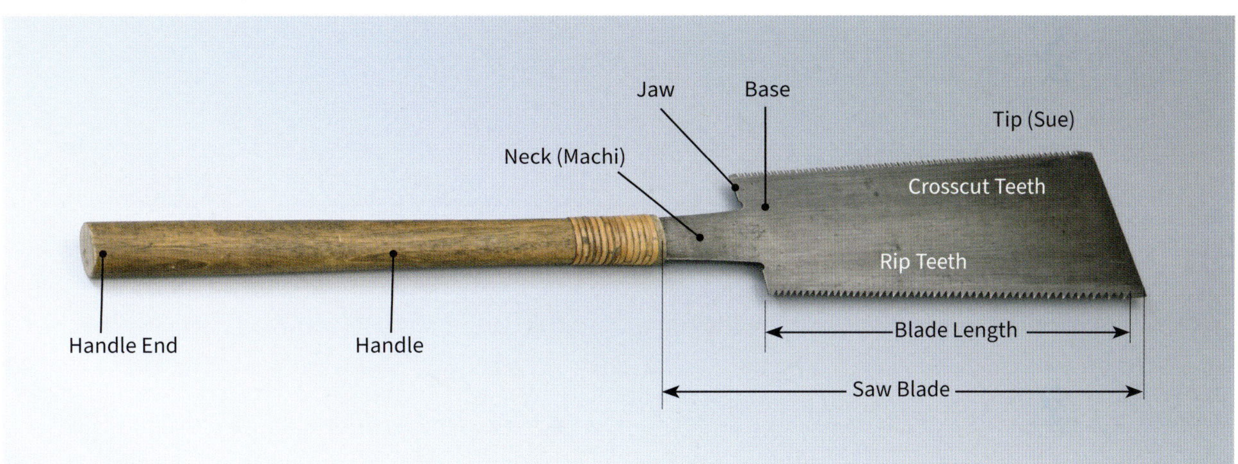

Classifications and Measurements of Hand-Forged Saws

While replaceable-blade saws display blade length in millimeters, hand-forged saws use the traditional Japanese shakkanhō system, with lengths expressed in sun (寸). For example, you may see measurements like "8 sun" or "9 sun."

However, these measurements do not correspond directly to blade length or total saw length, making things a bit confusing.

One sun is approximately 1.2 inches (30.3 mm).

You can remember that the indicated length is "blade length + 1 sun." So, for an 8 sun saw, the blade length would be 7 sun.

Regardless of the size, hand-forged saws typically have a similar number of teeth along the blade. As the sun increases, each tooth also becomes larger.

Sometimes, you'll also see the notation "sun ○ teeth," indicating how many teeth are embedded within one sun length.

Additionally, pitch (the spacing between each tooth) is sometimes displayed.

This notation applies only to crosscut saws with evenly spaced teeth.

Since rip saw teeth grow larger towards the tip, neither notation is applicable to them.

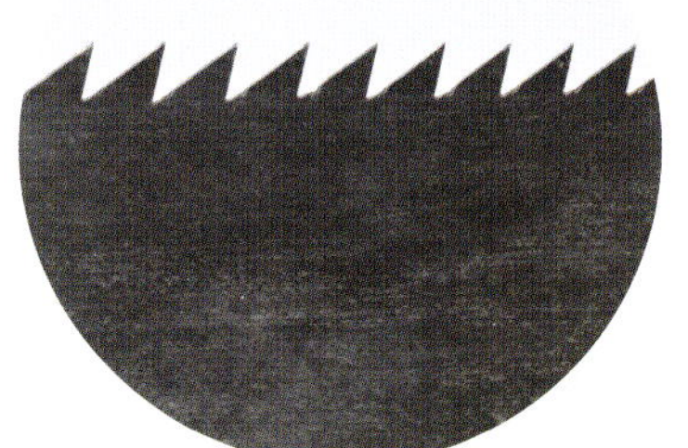

On one side of the double-edged saw is the rip saw, which cuts parallel to the wood grain.

The teeth of a rip saw are arranged in a straight line with nearly identical shapes.

CUTTING MECHANISMS

The Teeth of Rip Saws and Crosscut Saws Differ in Shape, Each Designed to Reduce Friction Resistance

Hand-forged saws come in two common types: rip and crosscut. Each has a different blade shape and a structurally precise design. They're also equipped with a feature called asari to prevent the blade from adhering closely to the material.

Rip Saws Are Like Chisels, Crosscut Saws Are Like Small Knives, Aligned in a Straight Line

The photograph on the middle left page shows a close-up of a rip saw blade, while the one below it shows a close-up of a crosscut saw blade.

The difference is obvious. The rip saw blade, which cuts parallel to the wood grain, has a simpler design than the crosscut saw.

The teeth of a rip saw are often compared to chisels, as the rear edge of the saw scoops out the wood like a chisel. These chisel-like teeth are arranged in a straight line.

Since the wood grain direction is softer and offers less resistance, a relatively simple blade design is sufficient.

Moreover, the teeth of a rip saw gradually increase in size from the base to the tip.

As you cut, the amount of wood removed increases, allowing the groove to be dug deeper—an intentional and well-thought-out design.

It's important to reconsider the perception that saws are merely hand tools with blades.

On the other hand, the blade of a crosscut saw is more complex than that of a rip saw.

Since crosscutting requires cutting perpendicular to the wood grain, the resistance is much greater than when ripping.

For this reason, the teeth of a crosscut saw are smaller than those of a rip saw, designed to

Crosscut saws are used to cut perpendicularly across the wood grain.

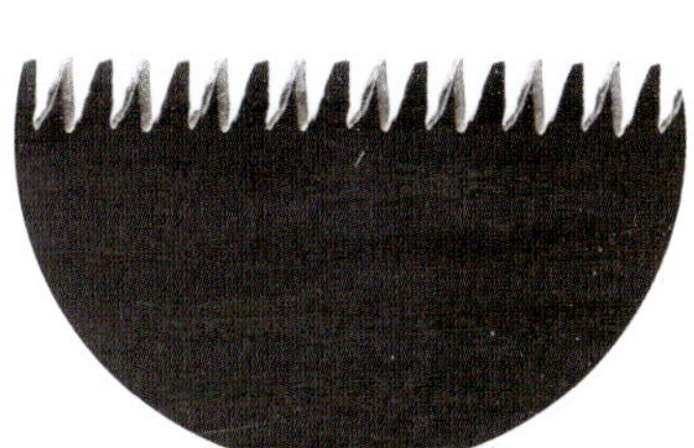

The alternating omote (front) and ura (back) sides form the structure of a crosscut saw.

make finer cuts through the fibers.

However, smaller teeth make the saw easier to use and produce cleaner cuts, though it requires more strokes to complete the cut. This balance of ease of use, cut quality, and cutting efficiency determined the size of the teeth.

In crosscut saws, the teeth are uniformly sized from the base near the handle to the tip, unlike rip saws. Additionally, the cutting edge is only present on one side of each tooth.

The two cutting edges on the sides of the tooth are called nageshi, and the slanted cutting edge on the top is known as uwame.

The side with the cutting edges is called the omote (front), while the side without them is the ura (back). These omote and ura teeth alternate along the blade, forming the structure of a crosscut saw.

While rip saw teeth are compared to chisels, crosscut saw teeth are often likened to small knives. The uwame cutting edge on the top also plays a crucial role in crosscutting, allowing the blade to penetrate the wood more effectively and reducing the effort needed to cut.

Have you now understood the differences between rip and crosscut saws?

Some may have thought the difference was only in the size of the teeth.

It is unknown when the "invention" of differentiating blade shapes occurred, but it likely emerged from the continuous dedication of blacksmiths.

There is also a saw called ibara-me (see photo on the next page), which has a shape similar to a crosscut saw.

Like the crosscut saw, it has cutting edges on both sides of the teeth but lacks the uwame at the top.

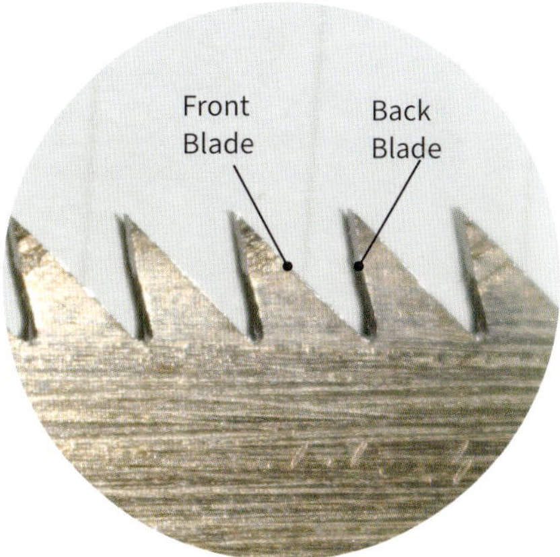

Rip saw blades have front and back edges, where each back edge scoops the wood like a chisel.

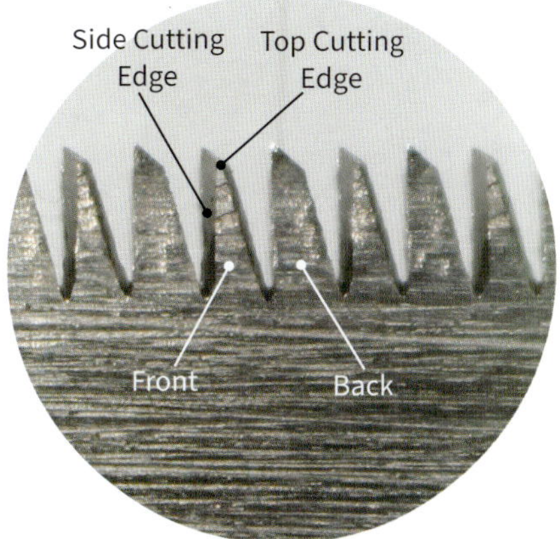

Crosscut saw blades alternate between omote (with three cutting edges) and ura (without cutting edges).

Ibara-me is considered a predecessor of the crosscut saw, and after the current crosscut saw was developed in Edo (modern Tokyo), it lost its prominence.

For this reason, crosscut saw blades are sometimes referred to as Edo-me.

Ibara-me is now rarely seen in the market, used only by some craftsmen for angled cuts or plywood work.

The close-up of a saw blade from above shows how the asari bends the teeth outward.

The Ingenious Structure of Using Alternating Saw Teeth for Smooth Cutting

The saw has asari. Not many people might understand what this means immediately.

Asari, also known as haba-kiri (blade setting), refers to bending the teeth of the saw alternately outward.

The name comes from its resemblance to the shells of a clam (asari), but unlike the clam, the teeth are staggered alternately.

Why is asari necessary?

If the cutting width isn't wider than the thickness of the saw blade, the blade and the material would stick together, making it difficult to cut.

Additionally, when cutting thicker materials, the saw might get stuck and be hard to remove.

If the blade thickness and cut width are the same, sawdust clogs the groove and cannot be expelled. Asari solves these problems, making it easier to cut with less effort and allowing sawdust to flow smoothly.

Both rip and crosscut saws have asari, and in double-edged saws, ensuring both sides have equal bend width is a testament to the saw craftsman's skill.

If the bend width is uneven, the teeth with a larger bend will catch on the wood.

There are also saws without asari.

For example, in woodworking, when inserting a wooden dowel into a hole, a small saw is used to trim the dowel flush with the surface.

This type of saw is valued because it does not damage the surrounding area, thanks to the absence of asari.

There are videos on social media showing how to adjust asari, but beginners should avoid attempting this.

If the asari is misaligned, the saw will no longer cut straight and may deform.

Saws encapsulate various wisdom and knowledge derived from the experience of craftsmen.

Have you gained a new appreciation for saws?

The ibara-me blade lacks the uwame cutting edge, making it ideal for diagonal cuts, often favored by professionals for specialized tasks.

A hand-forged saw, imbued with countless ingenious insights, becomes more cherished with every use.

In the past, stone axes (bottom) were used to cut down trees, followed by iron axes (top).

SAW HISTORY

The Emergence of Large Saws That Revolutionized Timber Processing and Architectural Styles

Saws were introduced to Japan quite early, but it wasn't until the 15th century that they began playing a prominent role in construction. Why did it take so long? The history of saws is deeply linked with architectural history. Let's explore this evolution.

A Supporting Role in Construction Sites, Further Hampered by Underdeveloped Iron-working Techniques

It's believed that saws were introduced to Japan from China during the late Yayoi to the Kofun period. However, the details remain unclear.

Saws have been unearthed from 5th-century Kofun tombs as burial items (see the photo to the right), confirming their existence during the mid-Kofun period. These excavated saws were small and likely used for crafting rather than construction. Since they were included as burial goods, they must have been quite valuable at the time.

Replica of a saw excavated from a Kofun-period tomb.
◎ Photo courtesy of the Takenaka Carpentry Tools Museum.

Wooden structures began during the Jomon period, continued through the Kofun period, and culminated in large buildings like Horyu-ji Temple during the Asuka period.

Although saws gradually increased in size and

were incorporated into construction, even in the Asuka period, they were not yet used for full-scale timber processing. In fact, even for monumental projects like Horyu-ji, saws were mainly used for adjusting the length of timber, serving a supplementary role.

So how were wooden planks made? Let's take a brief detour to explore this.

For felling trees, axes were used. Iron axes, introduced from the Korean Peninsula during the Yayoi period, greatly improved efficiency compared to the stone axes used before. Research suggests that iron axes were up to four times more efficient than stone axes for tree felling.

Once trees were felled, chisels and wedges were driven vertically into the wood to split it into blocks. This method was known as "split timber processing."

These blocks were then shaped into thinner planks using an adze and further smoothed with a yari-kanna (spear plane). However, this method made it difficult to produce thin planks. Thinning wood with an adze required considerable time and effort, which is why the walls and ceiling boards of structures like Horyu-ji were thick.

By the Kofun period, tools like chisels, adzes, and yari-kanna had already been introduced from the mainland.

Split timber processing, which began in the late Jomon period, surprisingly continued until the mid-Muromachi period. While vertical saws were introduced and used for timber processing, split timber remained the primary method because ironworking techniques were still primitive, resulting in poor-quality saw blades. Thin blades would break, while thick blades increased cutting resistance, making them unsuitable for heavy-duty tasks.

Nevertheless, saws gradually evolved. By the 13th century, leaf-shaped saws resembling halved leaves emerged. These adopted a pull-saw mechanism, whereas earlier saws followed the Chinese push-saw technique. This marked a significant turning point.

Until the medieval period, logs were split into planks by driving wedges into them.

An adze (right) for thinning planks and a yari-kanna (left) for finishing the surface.

By the 15th century, saws were specifically designed for pulling, similar to modern saws.

The Birth of Specialized Timber Workers and Front-Pulling Saws

Between the Kamakura and mid-Muromachi periods, large saws known as oo-noko (see photo below left) were introduced from China.

These massive saws required two people to operate, with the blade direction reversed in the middle. Timber was placed upright, and the saw was operated vertically, with one person above and the other below. Strings were attached on both sides of the saw blade to maintain tension.

Illustration from the 15th-century scroll "Sanjūsanban Shokunin Uta-awase" depicting two craftsmen working together to cut planks from large timber using a giant saw.

The oo-noko was powerful, capable of cutting thick logs vertically. Its arrival greatly improved timber processing efficiency and yield, eventually displacing split timber processing, which had persisted for over a thousand years.

This new timber processing method, known as "cut timber processing," allowed for the production of thinner planks. The Japanese term for sawdust (o-noko) originates from this oo-noko.

The ability to produce thin planks with the oo-noko significantly transformed architectural styles. During the Muromachi period, delicate structures like shoin-zukuri (a traditional Japanese residential architectural style) became possible, thanks to the widespread adoption of thin planks.

Moreover, cut timber processing made it possible to utilize previously difficult-to-work woods like twisted-grain pine and hard zelkova. This broadened the variety of usable timber species, introducing greater diversity into architecture.

However, the era of two-person oo-noko saws was short-lived. By the 16th century, single-person front-pulling saws (see photo on the next page) emerged, signaling a shift.

These front-pulling saws were a uniquely Japanese invention, made possible by advancements in ironworking. The main advantage was their ease of use compared to the two-person saws.

Replica of a large saw (oo-noko) on display at the Takenaka Carpentry Tools Museum.

Replica of a front-pulling saw on display at the Takenaka Carpentry Tools Museum.

Edo-period ukiyo-e depicting a sawyer using a front-pulling saw to process timber, a task requiring significant physical effort.

Front-pulling saws remained the primary tool for timber processing until the advent of electric saws in modern times.

As cut timber processing became more widespread, specialized groups of sawyers, known as ki-biki or oo-noko-biki, emerged, separate from carpenters.

In Edo-period ukiyo-e prints, carpenters and sawyers are depicted as distinct professions.

The Monumental Success of Double-Edged Saws: A Milestone in Saw History

During the Edo period, carpentry tools diversified. Specialized saws, such as those used solely for cutting grooves in door frames, were developed. Many specialized saws that still exist today were first created during the Edo period. Incidentally, carpenters were a prestigious and well-paid profession during the Edo period.

In the Meiji era, advanced foreign ironworking techniques were introduced. Until then, steel plates were handmade by blacksmiths from iron sand, but industrial advancements enabled the mass production of uniform, high-quality steel plates.

This progress in steel manufacturing led to the development of the double-edged saw, combining vertical and crosscut saws into one, during the Meiji period.

The double-edged saw, developed in the Meiji era, remains a standard in handcrafted saws today.

Despite the rich history of handcrafted saws, they eventually faced competition from electric saws and replaceable blade saws.

As a result, the hand-forged saw industry began to decline, facing challenges in finding successors. One can only hope that the value of hand-forged saws will be rediscovered and that they will find their way back into the hands of many once again.

SAW VARIATIONS

Saws designed for a wide range of professional applications, showcase individuality and precision. One of the fascinating aspects of traditional carpentry tools is the variety they offer. Saws are no exception, boasting a diverse lineup. Each one was created by craftsmen in response to the specific needs of their users, reflecting the depth of saw culture.

Functional Beauty and Presence: The Hard-working Saws of the Craft World

The featured saws belong to the craftsman Hitachi. They range from heavy-duty models to those used for fine work, offering a rich variety.

Today, with prefabricated construction methods becoming the norm, these saws are less familiar to the average carpenter.

Even more so for DIY enthusiasts, they might seem like relics from another era. Yet, their precise shapes and distinct aura command respect. Anyone who appreciates traditional carpentry tools would find them a joy to behold.

If given the chance, these are tools you'd want to hold and experience at least once.

LOG-CUTTING SAW

A saw specialized for heavy-duty tasks such as cutting logs and thick timber

This saw is characterized by a slightly curved blade and the absence of a notch at the heel. It is a robust tool used for cutting off the ends of logs and other demanding tasks.

Although it is a type of crosscut saw, its blade is designed with thorn-shaped teeth (ibara-me), making it suitable for diagonal cuts as well.

Standard sizes range from 13 to 16 sun (approximately 15.4-18.9 inches/39-48 cm), placing it among the larger saws.

Depending on the region, it is also known as hanamaru noko or senmaru noko. The name anabiki is said to originate from the Edo period, when it was used by specialist carpenters who built anagura—underground storage pits.

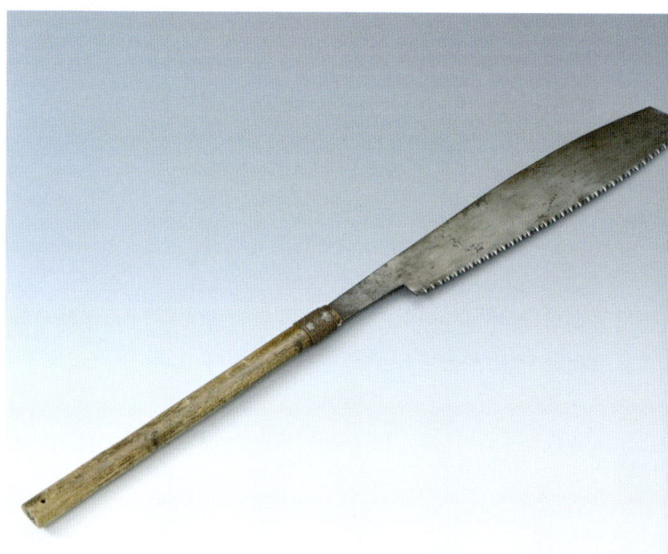

Thorn-shaped teeth allow powerful crosscuts and diagonal cuts.

ROUGH-CUT VERTICAL SAW

A single-edged rip saw favored by professionals for heavy-duty vertical cuts

Known among professionals as gagari, this rip saw features a handle attached at an angle. The slanted handle allows the user to position their body over the timber, making it easier to pull the saw during cutting.

It is designed for rough splitting, such as cutting logs vertically.

There is also a version with a straight handle, but this is typically used for smaller timber and is intended for finer vertical cuts.

The angled handle makes it easier to cut large timber.

CROSSCUT SAW

A standard tool every professional carpenter once owned for making cuts perpendicular to the grain

Commonly referred to as a kiri, this single-edged saw is designed exclusively for crosscutting, cutting perpendicular to the wood grain.

It is considered a standard among hand-forged saws. In the past, carpenters always carried this saw along with the gagari.

Compared to the crosscut edge of a double-edged saw, the kiri offers greater stability during cutting.

Standard sizes range from 8 sun to 13 sun (approximately 9.4-15.4 iches/24-39 cm), making it a medium-sized saw.

A staple for professionals, the hikikiri noko is designed exclusively for crosscutting.

BACKED SAW

A saw with an extremely thin blade designed for precise cuts and a beautifully smooth finish

The saw blade is exceptionally thin, ranging from 0.2 to 0.3 millimeters, and features a spine to prevent the blade from bending. The tooth pitch is about 1 millimeter, producing such a clean cut that no further planing is necessary. It excels in situations requiring precise and detailed cuts, such as finishing or detailed joinery work.

Due to the spine, it cannot fully cut through thick wood. The standard size ranges from 8 sun to 1 shaku (approximately 9.4–11.8 inches/24–30 cm).

This saw is designed for crosscutting and is reinforced with a spine to support its thin blade.

GROOVE-CUTTING SAW

When cutting long grooves in structures like door sills and lintels, the azebiki noko is used to make incisions on both sides of the groove, which is then deepened with a chisel

Commonly referred to as a kiri, this single-edged saw is designed exclusively for crosscutting, cutting perpendicular to the wood grain.

The outward curve of the blade makes it easier to make precise cuts on flat surfaces. It is also used to cut holes in thin boards. While there are single-edged versions, the double-edged type is more common. The neck of the saw is elongated for easier handling.

The curved blade of the azebiki noko is also useful for cutting holes in boards.

SHIPWRIGHT'S RIP SAW

The funate hikiwari noko is a type of rip saw used to thin materials by cutting away excess wood.

A saw originally developed by shipwrights for rip-cutting, recognized for its wide blade and robust appearance

Hikiwari refers to the process of ripping and thinning a piece of wood by cutting away unnecessary material. This saw was developed by shipwrights to level the joining surfaces of ship planks and later gained popularity among carpenters in the construction industry.

Due to its resemblance to a sea bream (tai), it is also known as the tai-gata (sea bream shape) saw. The blade is wide and commands a strong presence. Standard sizes range from 1 shaku 2 sun to 1 shaku 4 sun (approximately 36 to 42 cm).

The blade is designed for rip cuts.

CURVE-CUTTING SAW

The hikimawashi noko, capable of cutting curves, is a valuable tool for enhancing your DIY projects.

A versatile saw capable of cutting curves, making it ideal for intricate woodworking and DIY projects

Despite its delicate appearance, it's a fully functional saw. It features a thin blade with a single-edged crosscutting tooth pattern. The blade is inserted into a predrilled hole and used to cut along complex curves, making it highly useful for intricate woodworking projects.

However, due to its thin blade, it is not suitable for cutting thick materials. Various lengths are available, ranging from 6 sun to 1 shaku (approximately 7.1–11.8 inches/18–30 cm).

Although typically used as a pull saw, there is also a push-type variant known as the tsukimawashi noko.

Align your eyes, elbow, saw blade and marking line on the same axis.

Grip the saw by the handle's end, focusing on applying pressure with your ring and pinky fingers.

HOW TO SAW

Master the Art of Straight Cuts by Letting the Saw's Weight Do the Work

One common challenge for DIY beginners is cutting straight with a saw. What's going wrong? Where's the problem? Masao Nakajima from Kōshō Hitachi shares essential tips for success.

Maintain Proper Posture and Saw Without Applying Force

The first point to remember is the correct use of rip saws and crosscut saws. Using a rip saw to cut across the grain causes the teeth to catch on the wood fibers, increasing resistance. Conversely, while a crosscut saw can cut along the grain, it requires more strokes, and the cut surface tends to be rough.

With a double-edged saw, the side with larger teeth is for rip cuts—check before you start sawing. For diagonal cuts, use a crosscut saw.

So, what size saw should beginners choose? For general DIY projects that don't involve thick or hard materials, an 8 sun (approx. 9.4 inches/24 cm) double-edged saw should suffice.

Now, let's dive into Nakajima's expert advice.

"Before you start, always draw a marking line (sumisen), even with a pencil," he advises.

Hold the saw by the handle's end, but focus on gripping with just the ring and pinky fingers. The goal is to saw primarily with one hand, while the other hand offers only light support.

When positioning yourself, make sure your eye line, the saw's back, and the marking line form a straight line. Beginners often saw inaccurately because they view the cut from an angle, causing the blade to stray.

At the beginning of a cut, don't tilt the saw too much. Instead, use the base of the blade to start the incision. Placing the thumbnail of your supporting hand against the saw blade can help guide the initial cut smoothly.

As you progress, gradually increase the blade's contact area with the material by maintaining a gentle point of contact along the saw's length.

The key is to avoid forcing the saw with excessive pushing or pulling. This can cause the blade to heat up and warp.

"Let the saw's weight do the work. Always keep this in mind," Nakajima emphasizes.

If you follow these guidelines, Nakajima assures, you'll improve quickly. With practice and attention to these techniques, mastering the art of sawing straight is well within reach.

Use your thumbnail as a delicate guide for starting the cut.

Holding the handle too close to the blade destabilizes the saw and prevents straight cuts.

Start the cut with the base of the blade, then gradually incorporate the tip as you progress.

MAINTENANCE AND STORAGE

If the Blade Becomes Misaligned, Have It Professionally Sharpened: Proper Sawing Technique Is the Best Maintenance

If the blade becomes dull or warped, you'll need to take it to a professional saw sharpener. While blade wear is inevitable, warping is often due to improper handling. Make sure to practice proper sawing techniques regularly.

Steel Saws Are Prone to Rust, So Apply Oil and Store Them in a Dry, Well-Ventilated Place

Unlike planes, saws don't require extensive maintenance.

However, since they rust easily, it's important to lightly coat them with machine oil after use and store them in a location with good ventilation and low humidity.

Some people keep the anti-rust paper that came with the saw and use it to wrap the tool for storage.

Direct sunlight is not a suitable storage environment, as repeated heat expansion can cause the blade to warp.

Over time, the blade will dull, and when it does, sharpening by a professional saw sharpener is necessary.

If the blade becomes warped, it can also be repaired by hammering it back into shape. Improper sawing techniques are often a contributing factor, so it's worth reviewing your technique.

The cost of sharpening is reasonable, especially when you consider the craftsmanship involved. Due to competition with replaceable blade saws, prices are kept low. It's worth remembering that many sharpeners also work to preserve the tradition of hand-forged saws, often as a form of voluntary service.

After use, carefully wipe the saw with a cloth soaked in machine oil. Handle it with care, as you would any other blade.

At Nakajima's Kosho Hitachi, saws are stored in dedicated nokomaki (saw wraps) to protect them from rust.

The nokomaki used by Kōshō Hitachi to wrap saws. Affordable options are available, making them easily accessible.

JAPANESE GENNO HAMMERS: HAND-FORGED FOR PRECISION

The efficiency of transmitting applied force to the target is the essence of genno hammers. Blacksmiths devote themselves to refining this efficiency as they craft these tools. Their simple design belies their power, embodying why Japanese hand-forged genno hammers are truly works of art.

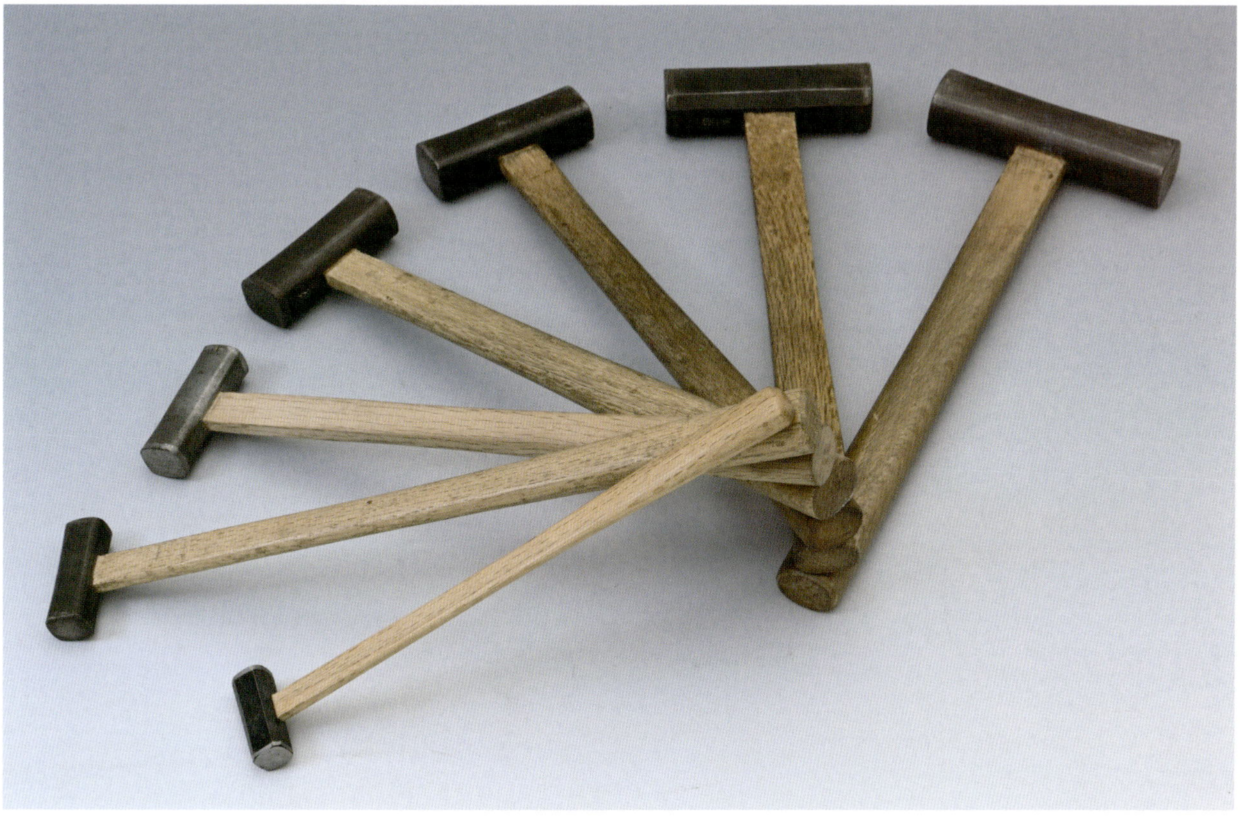

Grip the saw by the handle's end, focusing on applying pressure with your ring and pinky fingers.

GENNOGAKU: AN INTRODUCTION TO GENNO

A Hand-Forged Genno by a Blacksmith—Keep It as a Lifetime Tool

Once you experience the quality of a hand-forged genno hammer crafted by a blacksmith, you'll never want to go back to mass-produced versions. Surprisingly, they can be obtained at a relatively affordable price. But before making a purchase, let's explore the basics.

Pursuing the Ideal Form of Impact, Gennos Are Designed as the Perfect Partner for Chisels

The genno is sometimes written as gen'ō depending on the region. Its shape differs between areas like Kanto and Kansai, reflecting variations in local carpentry techniques—a fascinating detail. It's a vital tool, ranking just after planes, saws, and chisels among the three essential carpenter's tools. Naturally, it's also indispensable for DIY enthusiasts.

At this point, beginners might wonder: "Isn't a genno just a hammer?" While tonkachi is a common term for a hammer, genno is often classified as a specialized type of hammer.

However, carpenter tool expert Noboru Tsuchida challenges this notion: "A hammer is primarily used on construction sites for driving nails or bending metal. In contrast, a genno can also drive nails, but its main purpose is to strike chisels." Though similar in appearance, the two tools evolved separately for different purposes.

Unlike a standard hammer, the genno was designed specifically as a partner for chisels, with a focus on balance and efficient transmission of impact force.

Professionals don't use regular hammers to strike chisels. Standard hammers aren't designed for that purpose, and using one would lead to increased fatigue. Now you can see the difference.

From the Edo period to the mid-Showa era, specialized ana-daiku (mortise carpenters) carved mortise holes with chisels. In response to their demanding requirements, blacksmiths con-

Parts of the Genno

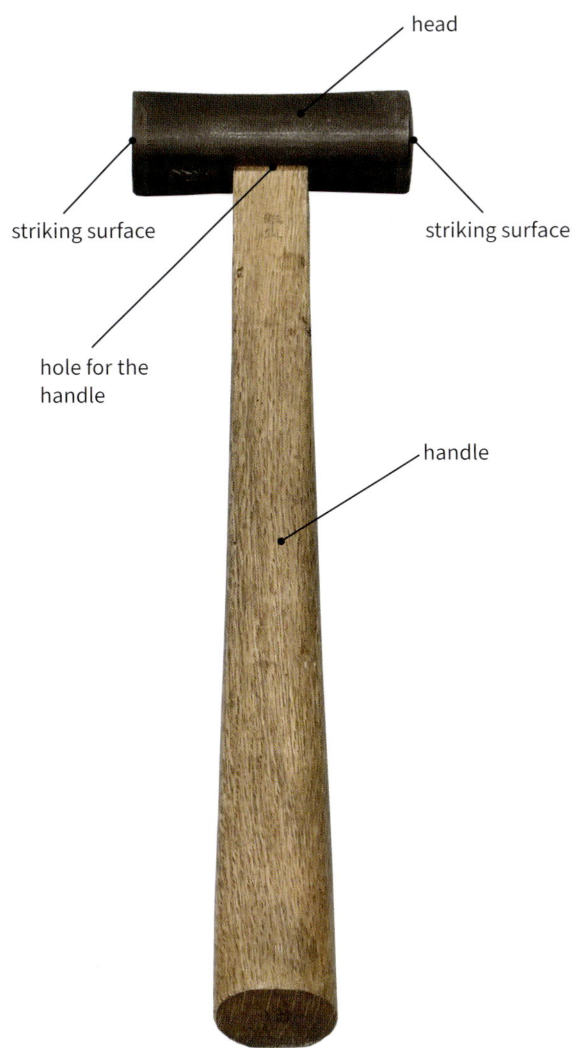

tinued to refine the genno.

Despite its simple form—a steel head with a handle—the craftsmanship extends to even the subtle details of the hitsu (the hole for the handle).

Interestingly, even genno hammers forged by top-tier blacksmiths are accessible at reasonable prices. With low wear and tear, they make for a lifetime companion—a tool you'll want to keep close for years to come.

The Popular Double-Faced Genno Comes in a Variety of Types

There are several ways to craft the head of a genno. Some are made entirely of steel (zengo), others have steel fused onto softer iron (hagane-zuke), and some harden only the striking faces through heat treatment. Due to fewer production steps, zengō types are generally more affordable.

The most common type is the double-faced genno, with two striking surfaces (koguchi) on either side of the head. Typically, one face is flat, while the other has a slight convex curve at the center.

This curved face, known as the kigoroshi-men (wood-tightening surface), is used for tasks like compressing wood or driving nail heads slightly below the surface. However, it's not used for striking chisels.

There are several variations of double-faced genno:

- The round-headed maru-genno is a well-known type. Interestingly, the shape of the koguchi differs between eastern and western Japan. In eastern Japan, an oval shape is common (kanto-gata or to-gata), while in western Japan, a perfectly round shape (Jigata) is the standard.
- Another variation is the square-headed shikaku-genno, favored by many professionals for its excellent weight balance during strikes.
- The octagonal-headed hakkaku-genno is versatile as it can also strike from the sides, making it useful in tight spaces. A hybrid type, the kata-hakkaku-genno, combines a round head with an octagonal head and is primarily used in central Japan.

One notable variation of the double-faced genno is the daruma-genno. It has a shorter, stubbier head, which gives it its name (daruma referring to the traditional round, stout doll).

With its center of gravity positioned lower, it's effective for strikes from a low angle. Choosing a slightly heavier version is recommended for optimal use.

From left: 20 monme, 40 monme, 60 monme, 100 monme, 120 monme, 150 monme, and 200 monme genno.

Genno Hammers are Categorized by Head Weight, Allowing Users to Choose Based on Their Intended Purpose

Various genno models are available, each with different head weights tailored to specific tasks. This level of precision is a hallmark of Japanese carpenter tools.

Just as traditional units like shaku and sun are still used for planes and saws, monme is also used for genno, such as "a 100 monme genno."

Since 1 monme is approximately 0.13 ounces or 3.75 grams, a 100 monme genno has a head weight of around 13.2 ounces (375 g). However, similar to how planes and saws are transitioning to centimeter and millimeter measurements, gram-based labeling for genno is also becoming more common.

According to Masao Nakajima from Kosho Hitachi, who assisted with product photography:

- For adjusting plane blades, an 80 to 100 monme genno is suitable.
- For smaller woodworking projects using mortise chisels, a 100 to 120 monme genno is recommended.
- For carving large mortise holes in beams with a striking chisel, a 150 to 200 monme genno is ideal.

Conversion of Genno Head Weight: Monme to Grams

20 monme	2.65 oz/75 g
40 monme	5.3 oz/150 g
60 monme	7.9 oz/225 g
80 monme	10.6 oz/300 g
100 monme	13.2 oz/375 g
120 monme	15.9 oz/450 g
150 monme	19.85 oz/563 g
200 monme	26.5 oz/750 g

Note: 1 monme ≈ 3.75 grams. Actual weights may vary depending on the maker.

For DIY projects primarily involving mortise chisels, Nakajima suggests that a 100 monme genno is the best choice, as it can also be used with planes.

In addition to double-faced genno, there is another type called katakuchi-genno (single-faced genno). One striking face is round, while the other side tapers to a point, used for nail setting.

- The katakuchi-genno is widely used in the Kansai region. Other regional variations include:

- Funate-genno (Iwakuni type) in the Chugoku region
- Funaya-genno (Hokkaido type) in Hokkaido and Tohoku Kyushu type in Kyushu
- Each type has subtle differences in design, reflecting local characteristics.

The katakuchi-genno can be seen as a hybrid between a genno and a traditional hammer, with a focus on driving nails.

Its center of gravity differs from that of a double-faced genno, leading to differences in handling. While experienced users may adapt quickly, for beginners aiming to strike chisels, the standard double-faced genno is the more user-friendly choice.

The single-faced genno, tapered on one side, varies by region.

Hand-Forged Genno Are Sold Without Handles, Posing a Challenge for Beginners

Hand-forged genno typically come without handles. This is because they were traditionally made for professionals who would craft their own handles. "Why not just buy a handle and attach it?" you might think.

However, the handles sold separately are often semi-finished and require adjustments for balance and length, typically measured from the user's elbow. Additionally, the handle must be shaped for a comfortable grip.

The handle should not be inserted perpendicular to the longer side of the head but rather tilted slightly toward the flat striking surface. This makes it difficult for beginners to attach the handle correctly on their own. In reality, it's more practical to find a shop that can attach the handle for you when purchasing the genno. While there is usually an extra fee for this service, it shouldn't be prohibitively expensive.

Lastly, let's briefly mention wooden mallets.

Wooden mallets have heads made from hard, resilient woods like oak or zelkova.

Although round heads are most common, there are also square, drum-shaped, and other variations. Wooden mallets are affordable and worth having in your toolkit.

Wooden mallets also come in various types tailored to specific tasks. For DIY enthusiasts, a round-headed wooden mallet is usually sufficient.

Named after the powerful hammer of genno zenji, filled with spiritual energy.

GENNO HISTORY

The Legend Behind the Name: A Monk Destroys a Cursed Stone with a Giant Hammer

Why is this particular tool called a genno? The origin of the name lies in a legend about a monk who shattered a cursed stone that brought harm to people, saving the populace from suffering. This strange tale takes place in Nasu, Tochigi Prefecture.

The Origins: A Great Hammer Wielded by a Monk, Later Adopted as a Carpenter's Term?

The story behind the name genno appears to originate from the Tamamo-no-Mae legend found in the Otogizoshi, a collection of medieval Japanese folktales. Over time, additional details were added to the story, and it gained popularity through kabuki and joruri (traditional narrative music), becoming a well-known tale by the late Edo period. In the late Heian period, a beautiful woman named Tamamo-no-Mae was beloved by Emperor Toba. However, she was actually a yokai, a nine-tailed fox, who brought disaster to the emperor.

When her true identity was revealed, the nine-tailed fox fled to the eastern provinces, eventually being shot with an arrow and dying in Nasu (now Nasu Town, Tochigi Prefecture). However, she was reborn as the sessho-seki (Killing Stone), a cursed rock that emitted poisonous gas, killing anyone who approached and causing great suffering to the people.

A high-ranking monk named Genno Zenji, who had founded Shigen Temple in Aizu, traveled to Nasu to seal the cursed stone. Possessing extraordinary spiritual power, the monk shattered the Sessho-seki into pieces with a giant hammer, allowing the people to live in peace once again. This is the basic outline of the story. It is said that the monk's great hammer, associated with Genno Zenji, came to be called genno or gen'ō.

Terms used only within specific groups are known as slang or jargon. For example, in the world of sushi chefs, shari (rice) and neta (toppings) are well-known examples.

The exact time when genno became a term is unclear, but it was likely created as slang or jargon, drawing from this famous legend. Like shari and neta, it gradually spread beyond its original context and became widely known.

Efficiently transmitting downward force to the chisel, a hand-forged genno is more than just a simple hammer.

Grip the end of the handle with the middle, ring, and little fingers, applying force only with these fingers.

If the balance feels off, you can adjust the handle by shaving it down.

A TAPPING GUIDE

If Held Correctly, This Tool Can Be Used with Minimal Effort (but It Shouldn't Be Handled Roughly)

A tool for striking with force and vigor—this is the general image of a genno. However, it's designed to allow for striking with minimal effort, making the genno a marvel of efficiency. Let's learn how to use this tool effectively.

Grip the End of the Handle with Three Fingers and Strike with Relaxed Shoulders

I learned how to handle a genno from Masaaki Nakajima of Koushou Hitachi.

The basic grip involves holding the end of the handle. The thumb and index finger should be held loosely, only as a guide, while the other three fingers should firmly grip the handle.

By doing this, the range of motion in the wrist is increased, and the movement becomes smoother, according to Nakajima.

I see, not only does this make it easier to

strike, but it also allows for better wrist snap, providing stronger force to the striking surface. Additionally, the handle doesn't wobble as much when gripped this way, allowing for more accurate strikes. Furthermore, this grip allows for an increase in momentum, giving added power to the strikes.

Now, although I recommended having the handle fitted by a professional, sometimes you might feel discomfort when striking with someone else's setup.

In such cases, Nakajima suggests shaving down the center of the handle slightly to improve the balance and feel.

The genno is used not just for setting chisel blades or striking chisels, but also for striking the ends of tenons to "kill" the wood, making it easier to insert the tenon into the mortise. The work can be surprisingly delicate. Though it rarely deforms, attention should be paid to the flatness of the striking face.

Be sure not to use the genno for rough tasks like prying or driving concrete nails. This is the key to making it last longer.

Once you're finished working, simply wipe it down with a cloth soaked in machine oil. That's all the maintenance the genno needs.

Lastly, let's touch on how to use a hammer for driving nails. Beginners often want to use a heavy hammer when driving nails, but Nakajima doesn't recommend it. This is because, when striking, the hammer may sway, preventing the nail from being driven accurately and straight.

"For long 5-inch nails (about 5.9 inches/15 cm), it's better to use a relatively light hammer, around 70 to 80 monme. This way, the nail will easily go into the material."

With a genno, you can apply subtle pressure for precise adjustments when setting a chisel blade.

The main use of a genno is still for striking chisels.

Strike the ends of tenons with the "wood-killing" face of the genno to make it easier to insert them into the mortise.

AN INTERVIEW WITH AN EXPERT

For DIY Beginners: How to Buy Hand Tools

I'd like to buy a carpenter's tool that was hand hammered by a craftsman but am reluctant to buy because of the price. If you've had these thoughts, you're not alone. Noboru Tsuchida, an industry opinion leader and owner of a carpenter's tool store, offers advice.

Buying a basic, inexpensive saw of decent quality

Let's start with saws. Replaceable blade types are gaining popularity, putting hand-forged saws at a disadvantage. Replaceable blade saws are reasonably priced. In contrast, hand-forged saws are often perceived as expensive.

Hand-forged saws are by no means overly expensive. For general-purpose double-edged saws, such as 8-inch or 9-inch ones, you can get a good quality product made by a proper craftsperson. This price range is perfectly adequate. In fact, the prices haven't increased for over 40 years. Due to the shift in demand toward cheaper replaceable blade saws, it's impossible to raise the prices.

So, essentially, top-tier products that should be sold at much higher prices are being constrained to this price range. While this is a good deal for users, it presents a harsh reality for hand-forging craftsmen.

Even the cost of resharpening when the blade dulls has remained the same as 40 years ago. There's no room for price increases. Considering the effort involved, it's practically volunteer work. The world of saw-making is tough indeed.

TSUCHIDA CUTLERY SHOP NOBORU TSUCHIDA

He's the third-generation owner of Tsuchida Cutlery. Known as a researcher of carpentry tools and blacksmith craftsmanship, he's written numerous books, including "Time and Blade," "Zeshu Chiyozuru," "The Modern Age of Craftsmanship" and "Cutlery: To Be." He's also a tool appraiser for TV Tokyo's "Kaiun! Nandemo Kanteidan."

A midpriced plane (kanna) is recommended. For chisels (nomi), no need to overspend.

When it comes to planes (kanna), replaceable-blade types aren't much of a threat. What does the product lineup look like?

For flat planes, they can be broadly categorized into four price ranges: basic, intermediate, expert-level, with the fourth category fetching exceptional prices appealing mostly only to collectors; those go beyond practical use.

So, which price range should one choose?

Midpriced implements work best. Even professional carpenters use planes in this range.

What about smaller planes?

Depending on the blade width, choosing the least expensive or a midpriced model would be a safe bet.

Next, let's talk about chisels (nomi).

In the past, there was a wide price range for chisels. Excluding mass-produced products sold at home centers, chisels like oire-nomi now cover the range from affordable to not so. Craftsmen who made very high-end chisels are no longer around; it's simply the way things have evolved.

So for oire-nomi, which level of product should one buy?

A modestly priced chisel is ideal as an entry-level option, as you'll need more than one

By the way, what's the difference between hand-forged tools and inexpensive mass-produced ones?

For planes, mass-produced products can't sustain long, continuous cuts and need to be sharpened frequently. Similarly, with chisels, it's difficult to use them for extended periods when digging mortises. It's best not to expect too much from them.

A top-quality product for next to nothing. Turn a masterpiece crafted by a renowned artisan into a family treasure!

Let's talk about hammers (genno).

There's a wide range of products available, but for example, the work of Hiroki Aida from Sanjo, Niigata—renowned as the best genno maker in Japan today—is afforable for any home hobbyist. With genno, you can obtain a top-tier product at this price point.

A small splurge can buy you a lifetime treasure. What's the difference between a top-tier genno made by someone like Aida and other hammers?

The hole where the handle is inserted is expertly crafted, ensuring that the force from your swing is efficiently transmitted to the striking surface. This precision is the essence of genno-making, and in top-tier products like those made by Aida, the level of accuracy is exceptionally high. Genno doesn't wear out much, so it's not just a lifetime treasure—it can be passed down for generations as a family heirloom.

For products of this caliber, you need to attach the handle yourself, don't you?

Finally, Tsuchida Hamono Shop is a salon for tool enthusiasts. If you're considering getting into DIY, it's worth visiting at least once.

TOKYO'S TSUCHIDA CUTLERY SHOP

TAKE A CLOSER LOOK

A Basic Introduction to Wood Science

We interact with wood through carpentry tools. However, without understanding the basic properties of wood, this interaction cannot be smooth, and the work won't progress well. So let's increase our wood knowledge. The more you know about the essential building block, the more enjoyable your DIY pursuits will become.

Each Board Has Its Own Warps and Bends and Every Piece Of Lumber Has Its Unique Quirks

When you visit a home center that sells lumber, you'll find a wide variety of boards. Just purchasing these is not enough to start a successful DIY project. You might think it's that simple, but while they may all look the same, each board is subtly different, with its own quirks like warping, bending, or twisting.

Moreover, the degree of deformation can vary depending on the type of tree and how the board was cut. Even if it's the same type of board, the level of distortion can change due to fluctuations in humidity, which makes working with wood tricky.

There are other factors, like the drying condition at the time of shipping and how the board has been stored, which determine whether the wood is suitable for the work at hand.

Wood is extremely delicate—almost like a "living thing." If you don't understand this, things won't go as planned.

Feeling a bit daunted? Don't worry. As long as you master the basic characteristics of the wood, you'll be fine. I'll guide you through it now. Some stores, unfortunately, place heavily warped boards in prominent spots, hoping to sell them to beginners. It's a troublesome practice.

To avoid falling into this trap, it's important to deepen your knowledge.

The Most Common Type Is Itame Boards, While Masame Boards Are Rare and Expensive

Trees that are felled in the forest are transported to a sawmill, where large electric band saws (band saws) cut the logs into boards.

During this process, three types of boards are created: itame, masame and shinmuchi (see the diagram above).

The most abundant is Itame, which is why it's cheaper than the others and is commonly used for building materials such as ceilings, wall panels, and flooring. This makes it the most popular type of lumber.

At home centers, itame boards are the ones most commonly sold. One of the big advantages of Itame is that it allows for the cutting of wide boards.

Masame boards, with their straight and beautiful grain, are used for high-end finishing materials, such as in doors or decorative pieces. The downside is that because fewer boards can be obtained from one tree, they are more expensive.

Shinmuchi, which includes the core of the tree, tends to split easily, so it's best to avoid it. Some shops may sell it mixed with Itame boards, so be careful.

To identify these three types, simply check the end of the board (see the diagram on the next page).

Boards of Itame Have a Front and Back. Learn the Difference and Use Them Accordingly

On Itame boards, the side closer to the heart of the tree is called the kio-ura (wood underside), while the side closer to the bark is called the kio-mote (wood surface).

The kio-ura side tends to have raised grain and is more likely to splinter.

For this reason, the kio-ura side is usually kept hidden, with its rougher side facing away from view.

While many pieces of work are designed to show the Kio-mote side, it ultimately depends on the piece itself. It's not a strict rule—just look at the material and decide accordingly.

Now, do you know that itame boards have an "up" and "down"? The side closest to the root of the tree is called the moto (beginning), and the side closer to the branches and leaves is called the "Sue" (end).

In the world of carpenters, there is an unwritten rule to use wood in the same direction it grew.

Though there is a superstitious aspect to this, if you were to use the wood in the opposite direction, you would be considered a beginner.

To distinguish moto from sue, look at the grain. The side with the wider grain is the Moto.

Warping and Bending Are Inevitable! Understanding the Warping Tendencies of Boards

The diagram above on the right shows how the end grain of different types of boards deforms. The most likely to warp or bend is plain-sawn (itame) boards, while quarter-sawn (masame) boards shrink uniformly, but the warping is less significant. Center-sawn (shinmochi) boards tend to swell at the core and are more prone to twisting. In DIY, avoiding these troublesome warpings depends on the type of board used.

Shops typically dry boards sufficiently to prevent warping, but because wood is a living material, it's impossible to entirely eliminate warping or bending. In fact, it's safe to say that it's impossible to find a board that is completely free from warping. While this publication won't cover it in detail, controlling warping and bending is one of the key pleasures of DIY. There are many tips available online on how to deal with distortions, so it's worth checking them out.

The above diagram explains the relationship between straight and reverse grain in plain-sawn boards. In carpentry, the term naomime (following grain) is often used to refer to the straight grain. If you handle the wood, you'll easily distinguish the reverse grain because it feels rough against the hand, making it easy to tell apart.

Wood Science Q&A

When DIY beginners visit the lumber section of a home improvement store, they may find themselves overwhelmed by the technical jargon and feel that the task is more difficult than expected. To help avoid such situations, this guide explains some basic terms you should know and offers tips for buying lumber without making mistakes.

Q What is SPF lumber?

A SPF is imported lumber from North America. "S" stands for Spruce, "P" for Pine, and "F" for Fir—three coniferous trees from the Pinaceae family. It's soft, easy to work with, and inexpensive, making it a popular choice for DIY projects. Most of the lumber sold in home improvement stores is SPF.

Q What is a two-by-four?

A It refers to lumber sized according to American building standards. All SPF lumber found in home improvement stores conforms to this standard. The name "two-by-four" (2×4) indicates its dimensions in inches, with a thickness of 38mm and a width of 89mm (see the table below).

Lumber Standards

Dimension	Thickness	Width
1 × 1	19 (approx.)	19 (approx.)
1 × 2	19 (approx.)	38 (approx.)
1 × 3	19 (approx.)	63 (approx.)
1 × 4	19 (approx.)	89 (approx.)
1 × 6	19 (approx.)	140 (approx.)
2 × 4	38 (approx.)	89 (approx.)
2 × 6	38 (approx.)	140 (approx.)
2 × 8	38 (approx.)	184 (approx.)

※Dimensions are approximate.

Q What are live knots and dead knots?

A Knots are classified into two types: dead knots and live knots. Dead knots are completely blackened, making them more likely to fall out, so it's best to avoid boards with them. In contrast, live knots blend with the surrounding wood and are less likely to fall out. They can even add character to the board.

Q What is KD lumber?

A KD lumber is kiln-dried wood that has been artificially dried. Compared to AD lumber (air-dried for six months or more) or green lumber (freshly cut and undried), KD lumber is less prone to warping and is moderately durable. However, it can be less flexible. Most of the lumber sold in home improvement stores is KD lumber.

Q What are engineered wood and plywood?

A Natural wood is often referred to as solid wood. Engineered wood is made by joining pieces of solid wood lengthwise or widthwise to create larger boards. Plywood is made by layering sheets of wood with alternating grain directions to reduce warping and bending compared to solid wood.

Tips for Buying Lumber

When purchasing lumber, ideally, choose boards that are straight, without warps, bends, or twists. However, this is not always easy. SPF lumber, which is widely available in home improvement stores, is soft and easy to work with but tends to deform easily. Even if the surface is polished and looks nice, warped boards may have limited uses.

Some people suggest bringing a steel tape measure or a convex ruler to check for distortions, but these tools can only measure length and not detect warping. Ultimately, visual inspection is your best option.

Look at the end grain to see if the board is curved toward the bark side. Then, inspect the length of the board for any bends or twists.

Place the board flat on the floor and move it slightly. If it wobbles, it indicates deformation.

While some stores sell lumber in bundles, these may contain warped boards or boards with knots. It is best to select each board individually. SPF lumber often has many dead knots and sometimes contains resin pockets (brown sap deposits), which should also be checked carefully.

Another important tip is to choose lighter boards of the same size. Heavier boards may not be adequately dried and are more likely to deform later.

CHARACTERISTICS OF COMMON BUILDING WOODS

• Japanese Cypress (Hinoki)
With its beautiful grain and ease of processing, hinoki has long been a staple of Japanese construction. Its softness has also contributed to the development of specialized woodworking tools. It is highly durable.

• Japanese Cedar (Sugi)
This cedar is the most familiar conifer in Japan. Its straight grain is another reason for its popularity. As a softwood, it is easy to work with and grows quickly, making it suitable for various structural components such as pillars, ceilings and doors.

• Japanese Red Pine (Akamatsu)
Known for its flexibility and resistance to bending, red pine has been used historically for beams in traditional homes. Its high oil content also makes it ideal for thresholds where smooth movement is necessary.

• Hiba (Thujopsis)
Primarily found in the Tohoku and Hokuriku regions, hiba is also known as asunaro. Its wood is slightly yellowish and emits a distinctive fragrance. Its antibacterial properties and water resistance surpass even those of cypress, making it a highly valued material.

• Hemlock (Tsuga)
Among softwood conifers, hemlock is strong and commonly used for structural components like pillars and foundations. Its striking grain makes it popular, but good-quality hemlock is rare, making it an expensive choice.

• Zelkova (Keyaki)
A broadleaf tree with a distinct grain, zelkova becomes glossy when polished, enhancing its grain pattern. High-quality zelkova is considered a valuable timber and commands high prices. It was commonly used in temple and shrine construction during the Edo period.

• Chestnut (Kuri)
Chestnut trees have been part of Japanese life since the Jomon period. The nuts are edible, and the trees are relatively easy to cultivate. Its excellent water resistance makes it a common choice for building foundations.

• Cherry (Sakura)
Valued for its intricate grain, cherry exudes a refined atmosphere and is often used for decorative elements such as thresholds and lintels. Its bark has a unique luster and is sometimes used with the bark intact for features like decorative pillars.

A Tool Tour: Japan's Oldest Blacksmith Town

In Miki City, Hyogo Prefecture, where the metal blade industry flourishes, many workshops produce hand-forged tools. For those interested in DIY, this is a town worth visiting at least once. As a former castle town, it also offers a serene travel experience.

The Miki Hardware Festival Draws Crowds to the Mecca of Carpentry Tools: Miki City

A major festival focused on carpentry hand tools that attracts 150,000 visitors from inside and outside the prefecture.

Located in the south-central part of Hyogo Prefecture, northwest of Kobe, Miki City is one of Japan's leading centers for the production of carpentry hand tools. Many workshops, including Jo-zaburo, featured in the opening article, are based here.

Although it's usually a quiet regional city with a population of about 73,000, the Miki Hardware Festival held on the first Saturday and Sunday of November each year brings in 150,000 visitors from across the country.

The festival's main venue is Miki-yama Comprehensive Park, where exhibitions, direct sales, and various events take place. Many visitors come to purchase hand-forged tools.

The Miki Hardware Festival bustling with visitors.
◎ Photo provided by Miki City General Policy Department

Traditional blacksmithing demonstrations, knife-making exhibitions, and more are also highlights of the event. In late May, another event, Kajidesse! ("We're Forging!"), offers hands-on experiences in Miki City.

This festival, organized by local blacksmith workshops, aims to showcase the charm of carpentry hand tools. Activities include a plane-shaving contest, saw woodworking classes, blacksmithing workshops, and log-cutting competitions, making it an enjoyable event for families.

For detailed schedules, check Miki City's official website. As the sacred land of carpentry tools, Miki City is also home to the Miki Municipal Hardware Museum in Uenomaru-cho, which preserves and shares the history and legacy of these tools. The museum features valuable exhibits that will captivate any carpentry tool enthusiast. Knowledgeable curators are on hand to provide detailed explanations.

On the first Sunday of each month, the museum holds demonstrations of ancient blacksmithing techniques in front of the building. Adjacent to the museum is the Kanamono Shrine, which enshrines three deities associated with metalworking. It is revered by those in related industries. If you visit Miki City, a stop at the shrine is recommended. The Fuigo Festival is held there annually on the first Sunday of December.

A flyer for the 2019 Kajidesse! event

The interior of the Miki Municipal Hardware Museum. A must-see for DIY enthusiasts, as it showcases the evolution of carpentry hand tools.

The Kanamono Shrine adjacent to the museum, enshrining the three guardian deities of blacksmithing, steelmaking and casting.

The Miki Municipal Hardware Museum was constructed in the Azekura style. It also hosts special exhibitions on hardware regularly.

MIKI MUNICIPAL HARDWARE MUSEUM

5-43 Uenomaru-cho, Miki City, Hyogo Prefecture
0794-83-1780
Hours: 10:00 AM– 5:00 PM
Admission: Free
Closed: Mondays (open on holidays, closed the following day), year-end, and New Year holidays
Access: About a 5-minute walk from "Miki Uenomaru Station" on the Kobe Electric Railway Ao Line

The Turning Point: Hideyoshi's Reconstruction Order, Leading to National Fame in the Edo Period

Miki's development as a sacred land for carpentry tools can be traced back to the Miki Battle in 1578. Toyotomi Hideyoshi, then under Oda Nobunaga, attacked Bessho Nagaharu, the lord of Miki Castle. After Nagaharu's defeat and suicide, Miki was left in ruins.

Hideyoshi ordered the reconstruction of Miki, gathering carpenters and blacksmiths from across Japan. After the reconstruction, these craftsmen spread nationwide, bringing with them the reputation of Miki's carpentry tools.

Thus, Miki blacksmithing gained fame, and during the Edo period, Banshu Miki's forged blades became renowned nationwide. Miki was lined with wholesalers distributing carpentry tools. A remnant of this era is the Kuroda Seiemon Shoten, a wholesaler near Miki Station. Established in 1765 during the mid-Edo period, it remains the only hardware wholesaler in Miki still in operation. The current owner, Kuroda Yasuyoshi, is the 10th generation.

The store, with its traditional Edo-period architecture, is designated as a national cultural property. A visit to this building offers a glimpse into Miki's prosperous past. Although it primarily operates as a wholesaler, they also sell directly to the public. To explore carpentry tools further, visit the Michi-no-Eki Miki in the southern part of the city. Its second floor is a hardware display and sales center, showcasing a wide array of hand tools made in Miki.

While tools can be purchased anywhere, acquiring them at the place of origin adds a special charm. While Jo-zaburo actively welcomes factory tours, many other workshops are also open to visitors. A quick online search can help you plan a visit. Though Miki is known as a town of carpentry tools, it also boasts many historical sites from the Sengoku period. The northern part of the city features the carbonated Yoshioka Hot Springs, along with numerous tourist attractions. Combining these with a tool-focused tour promises an enriching journey.

KURODA SEIEMON SHOTEN
2-3-26 Honmachi, Miki City, Hyogo Prefecture
0794-82-0009
Hours: 10:00 AM–5:00 PM
Closed: Weekends, holidays, year-end and New Year holidays
Access: About a 3-minute walk from Miki Station on the Kobe Electric Railway Ao Line

HARDWARE DISPLAY AND SALES CENTER
2426 Fukui Aza Mikiyama, Miki City, Hyogo Prefecture
0794-82-7050
Hours: 9:00 AM–5:00 PM
Closed: Year-end and New Year holidays
Access: About a 5-minute drive from the Sanyo Expressway Miki Ono IC. Located on the 2nd floor of Michi-no-Eki Miki.
◎ Photo provided by Mikiyama Co., Ltd.

JAPANESE CHISELS: THE KEY TO ADVANCED CARPENTRY

Despite being one of the three major carpentry hand tools, it's unfortunate that hand-forged chisels have been overshadowed by the widespread use of power tools in recent years. However, the sense of accomplishment when completing a joinery project solely with hand-carved techniques is unparalleled. The joy of DIY craftsmanship is deeply embedded in the act and art of working with chisels.

Various types of chisels were developed to achieve a wide range of cuts.

JAPANESE CHISELS: AN INTRODUCTION

Cutting Mortise Holes and Carving Grooves into Materials, Chisels Are the Most Diverse Hand Tools

They're used to carve mortise holes to join pieces of wood, cut grooves and even shave surfaces. Although electric mortisers and routers have gained popularity, hand-forged chisels excel in precise work. Let's rediscover the charm of hand-forged chisels.

Experience a Slow DIY Life with Hand-Forged Chisels Crafted by Blacksmiths

The chisel, consisting of a metal blade and a wooden handle, is simple in structure yet the most diverse among carpentry hand tools. Even the carving knives used in school craft classes are a type of chisel.

When carving a mortise hole, a chisel larger than the hole cannot be used, leading to the creation of various sizes. Additionally, chisels were developed to suit specific mortise holes, which contributed to the increase in types.

Although chisels have long been at the forefront of carpentry hand tools, the introduction of electric mortisers and routers has led to their decline.

In terms of efficiency, chisels clearly have a disadvantage. More woodworking classes now teach mortising using electric tools instead of chisels.

In today's world, where time performance (time efficiency) is valued, using hand-forged chisels while appreciating the craftsmanship of blacksmiths might be a unique and rewarding experience.

Some people mistakenly believe that the inexpensive chisels sold in home improvement stores are hand-forged. However, the blades on these chisels are mass-produced, not crafted by skilled chisel blacksmiths.

While they can cut well enough if sharpened properly, professionals point out that they lack toughness and wear out quickly compared to hand-forged chisels. Frequent sharpening is necessary, which is a disadvantage. Still, they might be useful as a secondary tool.

Like planes and saws, chisels also come with replaceable blades. These allow users to switch the blade material according to the task, and the blades can be sharpened as well.

The concept behind replaceable blade chisels is to make it easy to own chisels with different blade widths, making them worth considering as a secondary tool for those interested.

The World-Renowned Japanese Joinery System Born from the Evolution of Chisels

Japanese architecture is often praised for its intricate and diverse wood joinery, unmatched globally. While planes and saws also contributed to the development of wood joinery, chisels played the most significant role. Once you acquire chisels, you'll naturally delve into wood joinery, so let's briefly discuss it.

The technique of joining wood pieces is formally called "joinery" (tsugite shikuchi). A "joint" (tsugite) extends the length of wood by joining shorter pieces, offering the advantage of effectively utilizing shorter materials.

On the other hand, a "joint connection" (shikuchi) refers to the method of connecting two pieces of wood perpendicularly or diagonally, commonly used in DIY projects.

Wood joinery is essential because wood tends to deform. By joining pieces, they absorb each other's deformation forces, strengthening the overall structure and making it more durable.

This can't be achieved with nails or screws, as they eventually loosen under the stress of wood deformation. The photos above show only a small sample of joinery techniques. The variations are nearly endless, and carpenters of the past took pride in inventing their own joint designs.

The world of joinery is deep. Once you get hooked, there's no turning back from woodworking.

Mastery brings speed: mortise holes can be made quickly with a bit of practice.

LEFT **Collar joint (Eriwa Dume) / A robust joint**
◎ Photo provided by Takenaka Carpentry Tools Museum

RIGHT **Dovetail joint (Ariotoshi) / A classic joint**
◎ Photo provided by Takenaka Carpentry Tools Museum

LEFT **Housed scarf joint (Koshikake Kama Tsugi) / A traditional joint**
◎ Photo provided by Takenaka Carpentry Tools Museum

RIGHT **Housed dovetail joint (Koshikake Ari Tsugi) / A traditional joint**
◎ Photo provided by Takenaka Carpentry Tools Museum

On the left is a striking chisel, and on the right is a pushing chisel, both with a blade width of 8 bu.

Striking Chisels with a Hammer, Pushing Chisels by Hand

Chisels can be broadly divided into two groups: striking chisels and pushing chisels. In the photo on the right, the left is a striking chisel, and the right is a pushing chisel. Striking chisels are used by hitting the head of the handle with a hammer, primarily for carving mortise holes. The metal ring at the top, called a "katsura" (cap ring), prevents the handle from splitting under impact.

When people think of chisels, they often imagine striking chisels. Pushing chisels, on the other hand, have long handles and are used for finishing the interior of mortise holes carved with striking chisels or for trimming areas too narrow for a plane.

They are also useful for carving complex mortise shapes and tenons. Pushing chisels are operated by hand, either by pushing or pressing, and their handles are longer for better grip. The blade is also sharper than that of striking chisels. Since they are not struck with a hammer, they do not have a katsura.

In DIY projects, pushing chisels are less commonly used because finishing and side trimming are often done with striking chisels. However, for those aiming to take their skills to the next level, pushing chisels are essential tools. Some chisels combine features of both striking and pushing types, so it's important not to confuse them.

Chisels are sized based on blade width, typically measured in millimeters. However, traditional Japanese chisels also use the old Japanese measurement system (shakkanho), with units such as "sun" and "bu." For example, a chisel referred to as "1 sun 4 bu" has a blade width of about 1.67 inches/42.42 mm (1 sun = approximately 1.2 inches/30.3 mm, 1 bu = approximately 3.03 mm). Although the old measurement system can be cumbersome, understanding the conversions can deepen your appreciation for traditional hand tools.

The primary role of the striking chisel is to carve mortise holes, which is why it's built to be durable.

In areas where a pushing chisel isn't necessary, striking chisels are often used for finishing and trimming.

However, for deeper or wider mortise holes, finishing with a pushing chisel becomes necessary.

Once assembled, the mortise hole remains hidden from view, yet the chisel insists: "Carve it with care."

The upper edge is the bevel made from base iron, with a cutting edge at the tip. The flat underside is the back blade made of steel.

CHISELING MECHANISMS

The Superior Design of Hand-Forged Chisels that Enables Precision Cutting

Japanese chisels outperform their foreign-made counterparts in sharpness and cutting ability. This is because they incorporate unique features not found in other offerings. Let's delve into the secrets of this design using the common striking chisel as an example.

A Two-Layer Structure of Steel and Base Iron for Smooth Cutting

The manufacturing process of hand-forged chisels is quite similar to that of Japanese planes. It starts with forge-welding, where steel is placed on base iron, heated in a furnace, and hammered together.

However, unlike planes, which often use extremely soft wrought iron for the base, chisels typically use mild steel. Wrought iron is too soft and would deform under repeated hammering.

Most hand-forged planes use the Blue Paper steel series from Hitachi Metals, but chisels often use the slightly softer White Paper steel from the

The cutting edge made of steel shines brightly at the tip, while the upper bevel is composed of base iron.

Striking chisels, which are driven by a hammer, are mainly used for mortising.

same company.

The reason for this is that the high hardness of Blue Paper steel makes chisel edges prone to chipping under the intense blows of a hammer. In contrast, White Paper steel is more compatible with chisels, allowing for resilient and smooth cutting.

Why, then, do Japanese chisels have a two-layer structure of base iron and steel, unlike foreign chisels, which are typically made entirely of steel?

In forge-welded Japanese chisels, the steel forms the back blade and the cutting edge of the bevel, while the rest of the bevel, neck, and tang are made of base iron.

This structure allows the base iron to absorb the recoil from the material, protecting the hard but brittle cutting edge. This is a distinctive and superior feature of Japanese chisels.

Additionally, the steel encases the base iron in a U-shaped cross-section, providing a cushion-like structure that increases the overall strength of the chisel and prevents deformation from impact.

This well-designed system is the result of accumulated wisdom gained through experience.

In contrast, foreign chisels made entirely of steel have a higher recoil when struck, making them unsuitable for detailed work. This highlights the importance of the base iron in Japanese chisels.

The Unique Ura-Suki Mechanism for Maintaining the Flatness of the Back Blade

The two-layer structure, similar to that of planes, also facilitates sharpening. Pure steel alone would take much longer to grind. The ease of sharpening the bevel is a selling point of Japanese planes. Many foreign chisels do not have an ura-suki. The ura-suki is a shallow, elliptical hollow on the back blade, also found on Japanese planes.

The ura-suki was originally designed to reduce the area of the back blade that needs to be sharpened.

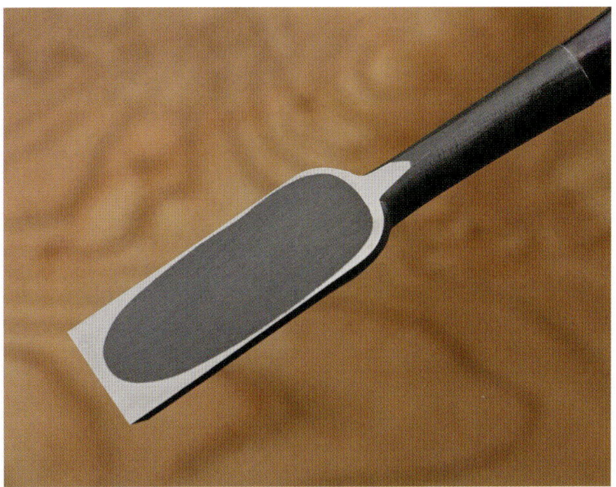

The back hollow (ura-suki) reduces the area to be sharpened on the back blade.

A chisel with three back hollows (san-mai ura), a hallmark of high-end chisels.

The left chisel, worn down from repeated sharpening, has lost even its back hollow.

The flatness of the back blade is crucial for chisels. When carving a mortise, the chisel follows the ink lines downward. If the back blade is not flat, the hole will not be accurate, leading to gaps in the wooden joints and compromising the structure's strength.

This is why the back blade is often referred to as a "guide" for precise cutting.

The ura-suki reduces the sharpening area, making it easier to maintain the flatness of the back blade. In this sense, the ura-suki plays a vital role in enabling precise cuts.

While most chisels have a single ura-suki, some have two or even three, as shown in the middle photo on the previous page.

The flat areas between the hollows are said to stabilize the blade during striking, but they require more craftsmanship and are typically found in high-end chisels.

The essence of a chisel lies in how efficiently it transfers impact force to the cutting edge.

Foreign chisels, on the other hand, are designed for processing hard materials, where the priority is making holes rather than precision mortising. The absence of a two-layer structure and ura-suki in foreign chisels reflects this difference in natural conditions and woodworking priorities.

The chisel used in China has a wooden handle inserted into a socket, designed for processing hard materials.

◎ Photo courtesy of Takenaka Carpentry Tools Museum

Efficient Power Transmission from the Head to the Cutting Edge

The power applied to the head of the chisel by a hammer travels through the handle, neck, and blade, finally reaching the cutting edge.

The key lies in the tapering shape from the handle to the tang. Reducing the cross-sectional area increases the power per unit area, making it an excellent system for transmitting energy from a mechanical perspective.

The chisel in the photo on the right is a socket-type used in China. The neck is shaped like a socket, into which a wooden handle is inserted. This is known as the socket type or fukuro-shiki.

In contrast, Japanese chisels commonly used today insert the tang into a hole in the handle.

Chisel Part Names (Back Blade Side)

※The terms "front" (omote) and "back" (ura) for chisel blades are not originally formal designations. However, they have become commonly used due to their adoption in educational materials, and this book follows the same convention.

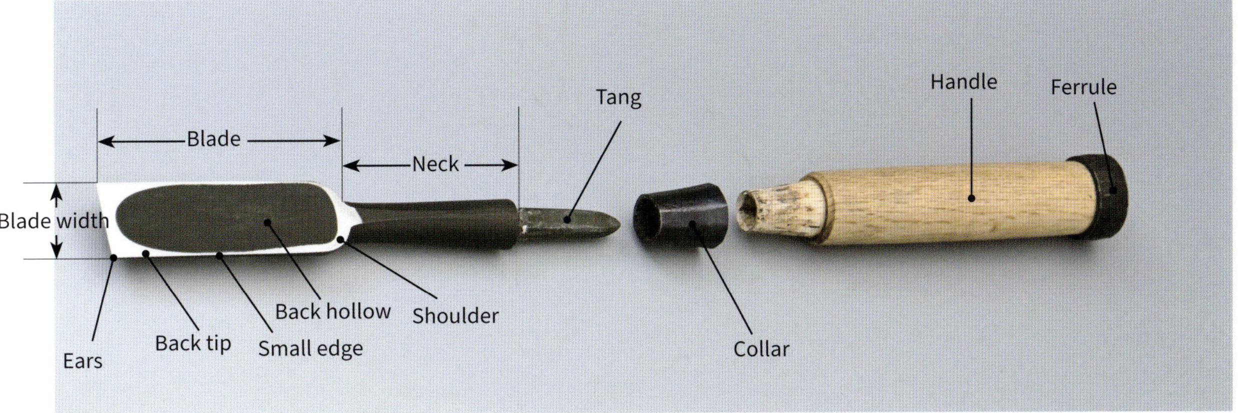

This is known as the tang type or kukisiki.

In Japan, both socket and tang types were used in the past, but the tang type became standardized during the medieval period.

Additionally, while Japanese chisels now have single-edged blades, double-edged chisels were also used before the medieval period.

The Japanese preference for tang and single-edged chisels stems from their suitability for precision work. The desire to continually improve and do better work is a philosophy deeply embedded in Japanese craftsmanship, and it is evident in chisels as well.

When you hold a hand-forged chisel, you can truly feel this spirit.

Japanese chisels are indeed exceptional.

Chisel Part Names (Bevel Side)

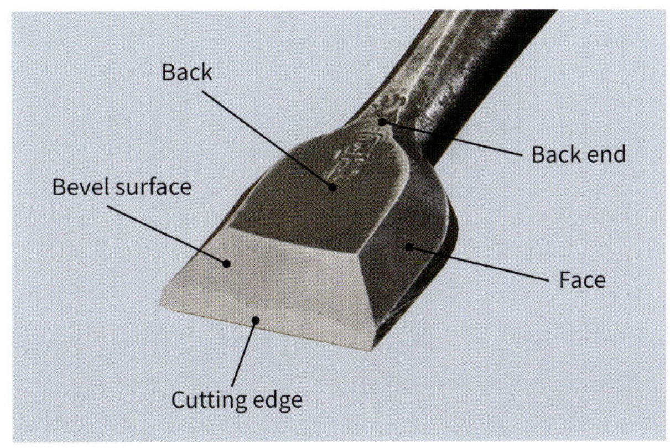

TIPS

Respect for Blacksmiths: A Chisel's New Life Even After Wear

While unthinkable at the DIY level, professional chisels, subjected to hard work and frequent sharpening, eventually lose their original shape.

At Kosho Hitachi, which assisted in this shoot, such chisels are not discarded but repurposed for different uses, allowing them to continue serving.

These chisels, crafted with great care by blacksmiths, deserve our respect. This attitude is something worth emulating.

A worn-down chisel was repurposed into a pointed chisel for pushing cuts.

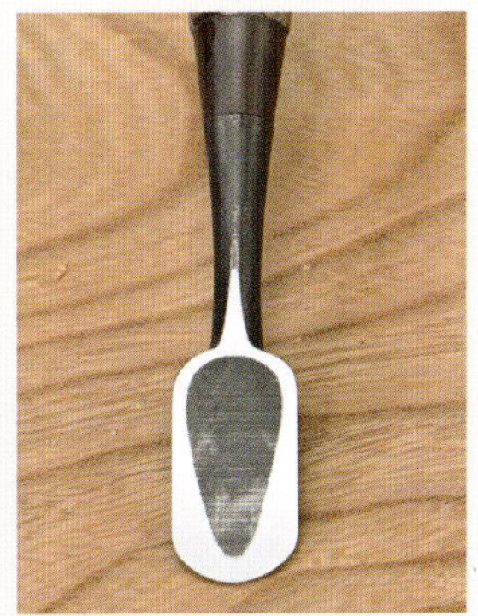

The blade was rounded to facilitate easy insertion into materials.

CHISEL HISTORY

The Transformation of Chisels Over 2,000 Years Has Been Driven by the Pursuit of Sharper Cutting

While the basic shape of chisels is said to have remained unchanged, they've undergone numerous transformations to reach their current form. Chisels were introduced to Japan during the Yayoi period. Let's take a quick look at their history from then to now.

Iron Chisels Arrived in the Yayoi Period, Leading to the Construction of Large Buildings with Joints

Copper chisels have been unearthed from Egyptian ruins dating back to 3000 BCE, indicating humanity's long relationship with metal chisels. In Japan, iron chisels were introduced from China during the Yayoi period. This period saw the construction of large buildings with complex joints, largely thanks to the introduction of iron chisels capable of mortise work. In the Kofun period, woodworking tools were often buried as grave goods in the tombs of chieftains. Excavations have revealed chisels with wide blades and shoulders, which were absent in the Yayoi period.

The significant improvement in iron forging techniques enabled these changes in design. Additionally, both socket-type chisels, where the blade is attached to a hollow handle, and tang-type chisels, where the blade is inserted into the handle, have been found in burial mounds, indicating that both types coexisted. These two types can be seen as the precursors to striking chisels and paring chisels, though their exact use in the Kofun period remains speculative. Another innovation was the ferrule placed over the striking end of the chisel handle to prevent splitting. This feature appeared between the Nara and Heian periods, though the details are unclear.

A chisel excavated from a 5th-century burial mound (reconstructed). The one on the right is a socket-type, and the one on the left is a tang-type.

◎ Photo courtesy of Takenaka Carpentry Tools Museum

A reconstructed ancient chisel based on blade marks found on old timber from Horyu-ji Temple.

◎ Photo courtesy of Takenaka Carpentry Tools Museum

A reconstructed 13th-century double-edged chisel.
◎ Photo courtesy of Takenaka Carpentry Tools Museum

A carpenter striking a chisel, depicted in "Imayo Shokunin Tsukushi Hyakunin Isshu" (mid-Edo period, by Kondo Kiyoharu). At the time, carpenters were highly paid and the profession considered prestigious.

Transition to Single-Edged Tang Chisels in the Muromachi Period, Leading to the Current Style

As mentioned in the section on saws, Japan used the uchi-wari method of splitting logs for lumber since the Jomon period.

Chisels, in addition to wedges, were used for splitting logs.

In other words, chisels were not only used for carving mortises but also for driving vertically into logs during splitting.

For such splitting work, double-edged chisels, with blades on both sides of the cutting edge, were commonly used.

The shift to single-edged chisels occurred during the Muromachi period, likely due to changes in lumbering techniques.

Around the 15th century, large saws for two-person use, introduced from China, became widespread.

This advancement led to more efficient lumbering techniques, reducing the need to split logs with chisels. Sawing and splitting wood expanded, and chisels were increasingly used primarily for mortising.

As chisels became more specialized for joint work, single-edged designs became the norm, and tang-type handles, which allowed for more precise work, gained popularity.

By the Muromachi period, the standard chisel design had largely taken shape.

This coincided with the rise of delicate architectural styles such as sukiya-zukuri, which required precise craftsmanship. Chisels evolved to meet these demands for finer cutting.

The final technical innovation was the introduction of ura-suki (a hollow grind on the back of the blade), which became common in the late Edo period.

Although now a distinctive feature of Japanese chisels, its adoption came relatively late.

The Edo period saw the diversification of woodworking tools, with many specialized tools emerging, including chisels for specific tasks like kote-nomi, designed for cleaning the bottom of grooves.

In the Edo period, mortise carpenters (ana-daiku or mortise specialists) became a distinct profession, separate from general carpentry.

At their peak, these craftsmen could carve 40 mortises in a single day.

However, mortise carpenters disappeared from construction sites in the 1960s, largely due to the widespread adoption of electric mortisers.

This marked a symbolic decline in the 2,000-year history of hand-forged chisels.

A set of mortise chisels. The difference in the size of the back blade is clearly visible.

JAPANESE CHISEL VARIATIONS

Upgrade Your DIY Repertoire with Versatile and Unique Chisels

Among traditional woodworking tools, chisels are the most diverse, and many are difficult to identify by appearance alone. However, incorporating them into your work guarantees an elevated DIY experience. Let's explore the world of chisels.

From Mortise Carving to Finishing: The Era of Mortise Chisels

In the world of chisels, hon-tataki-nomi (heavy-duty chisels) once held the status of the ultimate tool.

With thick blades and long handles and necks, they were built for strength, used for rough work such as digging deep, wide mortises in structural materials like pillars and beams.

The primary users of hon-tataki-nomi were specialized craftsmen known as ana-daiku or mortise carpenters, whose trade dates back to the Edo period.

However, by the 1960s, the mechanization of construction pushed ana-daiku out of job sites, reducing the prominence of hon-tataki-nomi.

Taking their place were oiire-nomi (inset chisels). Also known as ōire-nomi, these chisels are designed for finer work such as furniture-making. Compared to hon-tataki-nomi, they have thinner blades and shorter handles and necks.

This shift in focus to smaller-scale projects prompted the rise of oiire-nomi as the go-to tool. Oiire-nomi was invented by a blacksmith named Kunikazu in Tokyo's Hatchobori district at the beginning of the Meiji era as a miniature version of the tataki-nomi.

It quickly became a standard and remains the most recognized chisel today, even in DIY circles.

They are typically sold in sets of ten but can also be purchased individually. A good starting point is a gobu-nomi (approximately 0.6 inches/15mm), with additional sizes acquired as needed.

Taking Your DIY Projects to the Next Stage with New Chisels

With a selection of oiire-nomi, a wide range of woodworking projects becomes possible. Creating joints and mortises will enable a more fulfilling DIY life.

That much is certain.

However, adding a different type of chisel, such as a shinogi-nomi (ridge chisel), can make precise dovetail joints achievable, further enhancing your projects.

Incidentally, dovetail joints involve using mortises and tenons that spread outward like an inverted V, resembling an ant's antennae.

This principle applies to other chisels as well. Each new chisel opens up a new chapter in your DIY journey.

What a wonderful experience that is.

Below are some of the key players in the world of chisels.

But this is not all. There are countless other fascinating chisels waiting to be discovered.

Lastly, let's not forget the dedication of the blacksmiths who handcraft these tools, enabling exceptional woodworking.

With that in mind, step into the world of unique chisels.

OIIRE-NOMI

From Mortise Digging to Finishing Cuts: Beginners Should Start with Oiire-Nomi

Oiire-nomi is the standard chisel and the first tool DIY enthusiasts should consider. A typical set consists of 10 chisels with blade widths ranging from 1 bu (approximately 0.1 inch/3mm) to 1 sun 4 bu (approximately 1.65 inches/42mm). The specific sizes you need depend on your project, but many people tend to start with chisels of 3 bu (0.35 inches/9mm), 5 bu (0.6 inches/15mm) and 8 bu (0.94 inches/24mm). Additionally, a 1 bu-nomi (0.1 inch./3mm) is useful for adjusting the press grooves on a plane.

MIDDLE STRIKING CHISELS

For those aiming for large-scale DIY projects, this chisel serves as an intermediate between the main striking chisel and the mortise chisel.

In some regions, it is referred to as "half-striking." It fills the gap between the heavy-duty main striking chisel, designed for rough work, and the mortise chisel, which is more suited for fine joinery. With its strong professional orientation, it is recommended for DIY enthusiasts tackling larger projects rather than the mortise chisel. Blade widths vary widely, from 0.1 inch (3 mm) to 1.9 inches (48 mm).

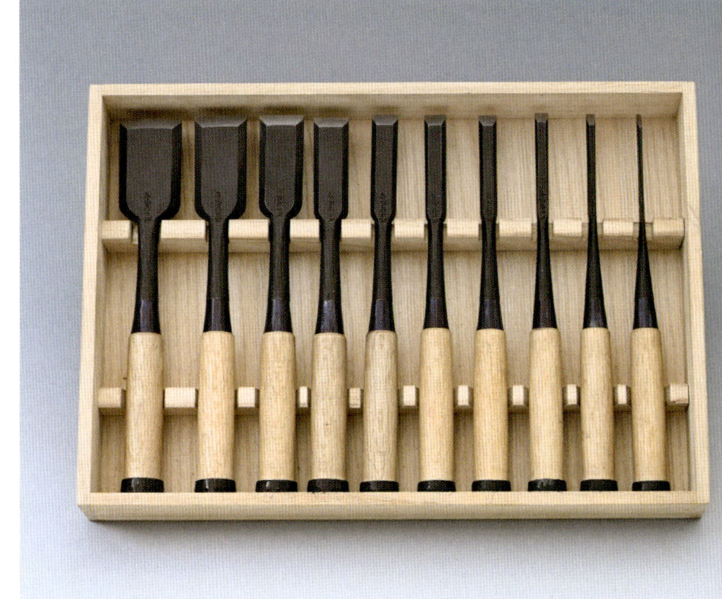

The photo on the left shows a set of 10, but like mortise chisels, it can also be purchased individually.

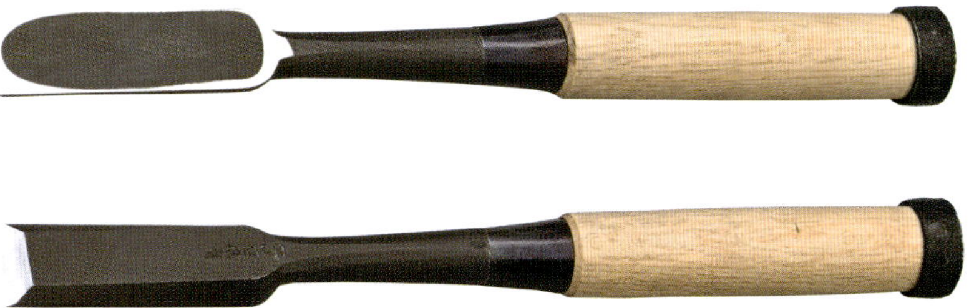

The middle striking chisel is built with a slightly longer and sturdier blade and neck compared to the mortise chisel.

TIPS

The "Neck-Cutting Chisel" is a Peculiar Tool with a Rather Ominous Name and It Lacks a Handle

This chisel is used when fitting floorboards into an upright column. Two cuts are made into the column with a saw, and the chisel is struck with a mallet to carve out material, creating a gap for the floorboards to fit into. The name comes from the act of cutting into the column as if severing it. It's also known as a floor-fitting chisel. Its simple structure without a handle allows for horizontal striking. Various blade widths are available, and it is a favored tool among carpenters.

It doesn't have a handle, as it would interfere with horizontal striking.

RIDGE CHISELS

A versatile chisel that's essential for precise finishing in sharp corners and fine detail work.

The blade has a triangular cross-section. It can reach and cut into acute corners where thicker, high-backed mortise chisels cannot. It is particularly well-suited for dovetail joints. Additionally, it is ideal for delicate and intricate work, making it a valuable addition for expanding your joinery possibilities. Blade widths typically range from 0.1–1.2 inches (3–30 mm). Both striking chisel and push chisel types are available on the market.

The image shows a striking chisel type on top and a push chisel type below. The push chisel type is more commonly used.

TROWEL CHISELS

With its bent neck and distinctive shape, this chisel excels at finishing the bottoms of grooves.

The name derives from its resemblance to a plastering trowel. It is a push chisel used for bottom finishing, such as in dovetail grooves. The bent neck prevents the user's hand from obstructing the work. It can also be used to reach and cut into the very end of grooves, expanding the range of tenon hole excavation. The cross-section is often triangular, and a variety of blade widths are available.

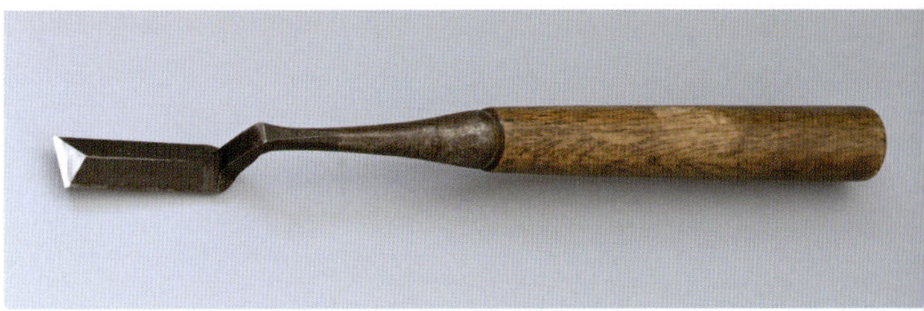

While primarily designed for cleaning out groove bottoms, the trowel chisel is also invaluable for other fine finishing tasks.

PUSH CHISELS

Acquire a push chisel and master surface finishing—it's also effective for trimming the sides of tenons and mortises

The push chisel is designed to trim and finish in narrow spaces where a plane cannot be used. It's perfect for finishing tenon holes and tenons. Once you have one, you can achieve professional-level craftsmanship. However, some might find the longer handles and necks of certain types to be over-spec for DIY projects. For those individuals, a thin chisel of the same type is recommended. Its flat, thin blade tip can handle finishing even in very tight spaces.

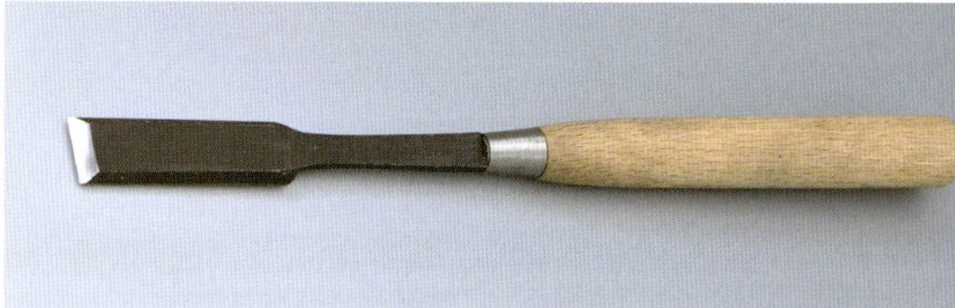

Thin chisels have shorter handles and necks compared to standard push chisels, making them easier to handle in terms of size.

OUTER ROUND CHISELS

A specialized striking chisel designed for professional use, with the entire back blade shaped into a curved surface

This chisel features a protruding curved cutting edge, used for processing attachment points on round posts or logs. Various sizes are available, with differences in blade width and curvature to suit specific purposes. Although it's a tool primarily used by professionals, it can be adapted for various DIY purposes with some creativity. Additionally, there is a type called the inner round chisel (uchi maru nomi), where the blade curves inward.

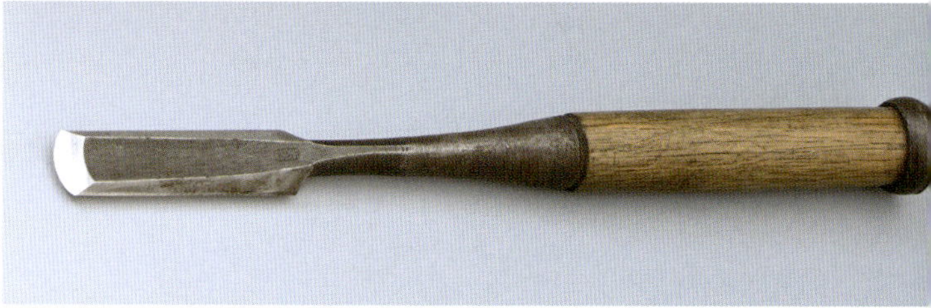

The back side of the blade on the striking chisel type of outer round chisel is finished with a curved surface.

REVERSE TROWEL CHISELS

A special striking chisel with a neck bent in the opposite direction from a trowel chisel, used for trimming the neck of columns

Like the neck-cutting chisel shown on page 116, this tool is used to cut the sides of columns and fit floorboards. Its neck is bent toward the hollow-ground side, opposite to the trowel chisel. While the trowel chisel is a push chisel, this one is a striking chisel. The photo shows a reverse trowel chisel made by modifying a mortise chisel, crafted by artisan Hitachi. Reverse trowel chisels are produced in limited quantities, making them difficult to obtain. They are entirely professional-grade tools.

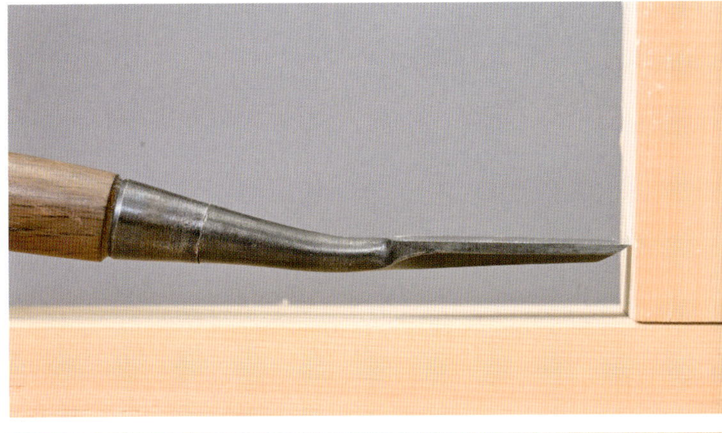

The reverse trowel chisel has a slightly bent neck and was created by modifying a mortise chisel.

SWORD POINTS

It resembles a small knife but is a fully functional chisel, complete with a hollow-ground back and an extremely sharp sword-like blade

This chisel is used to finish flat surfaces in places where a plane cannot be applied. With its hollow-ground back, it belongs to a different category than a small knife. To make it easier to shave, the handle is slightly elevated. The tool is similar in shape to a shirobiki (a marking knife used for cutting guide lines in wood), but its function is entirely different. Various blade widths and lengths are available on the market, but it's also possible to substitute a standard chisel by sharpening its tip into an inverted V-shape.

The sword-point chisel trims and finishes the surface of materials, with a hollow-ground back for added precision.

Specialty Chisels: A Gallery

Among the many chisels, we've collected some rare ones you don't come across everyday. Let's take a gallery walk through some our prized specimens.

MUKO-MACHI CHISEL

A small chisel used for drilling holes in fittings. It is also called a mukou-ku chisel. The cross section of the tip and neck is square, and there is no difference in width between the tip and neck. The blade width ranges from 5.5 to 6 microns. It is also called a joiner's chisel because it plays a leading role in the manufacture of fittings.

TWO CHISELS

It's a kind of mukaiwai chisel that can dig parallel holes for fittings at the same time. For this purpose, the tip of the chisel is divided into two halves. The blade width is generally 2.5 mm, and the distance between blades is 1.5 mm, 2.5 mm, and 2.5 mm. It is difficult to manufacture and is a product that makes chisel smiths weep.

TSUBOMARU CHISEL

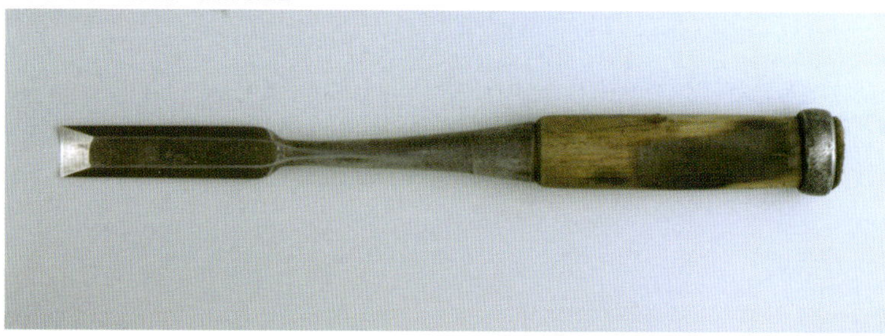

It's a kind of round chisel with a semicircular hollow cross section at the tip and used for finishing curved surfaces. Although there is an uramaru chisel of similar shape, the cutting edge of the uramaru chisel is round and curved, whereas the cutting edge of the tsubomaru chisel is set in a straight line. The standard blade width is three minutes to one inch.

GUARD CHISEL

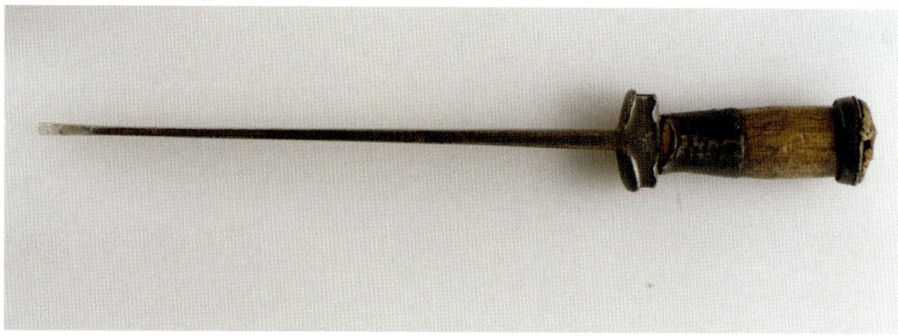

When large nails are to be hammered into a material, this chisel is used to pre-drill holes. The sword mount, from which the name of the chisel derives, has a sword-like projection under the handle for striking the chisel with a genno to remove the chisel. There are two types of sword: double-edged and single-edged. There are also double-edged and single-edged cutting edges.

CHISEL FOR BORING

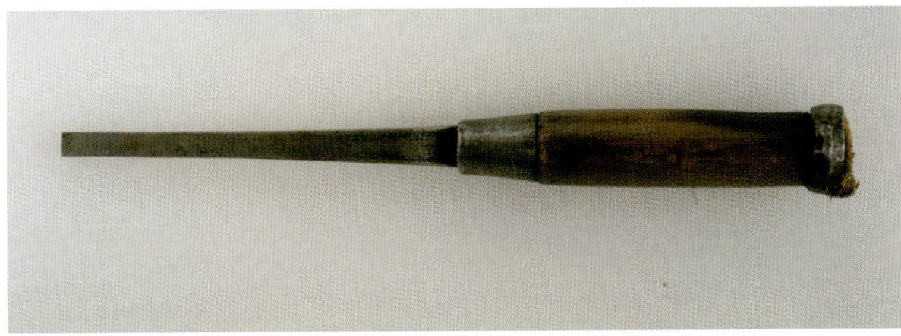

A great tool to choose when digging a hole. A hole is dug from both sides until it is nearly half full, and then this chisel is used to punch through the hole from one side. The tip of the chisel has no blade and is rectangular in shape. There is also a type with a V-shaped incision at the tip.

BOTTOM CHISEL

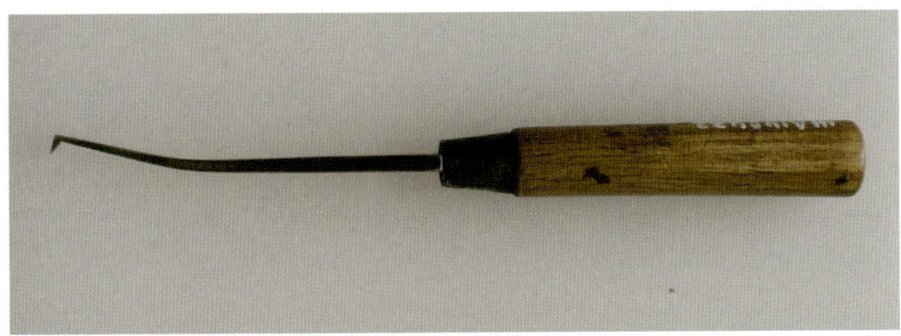

The bottom of a hole that is not penetrated is difficult to cut cleanly. The chisel is inserted into the hole, and while pulling the chisel forward, the cutting edge scrapes off the shavings. The characteristic of this chisel is that its neck is bent in the middle. This chisel is also known as a rake-out or shavings removal chisel.

HARPOON CHISEL

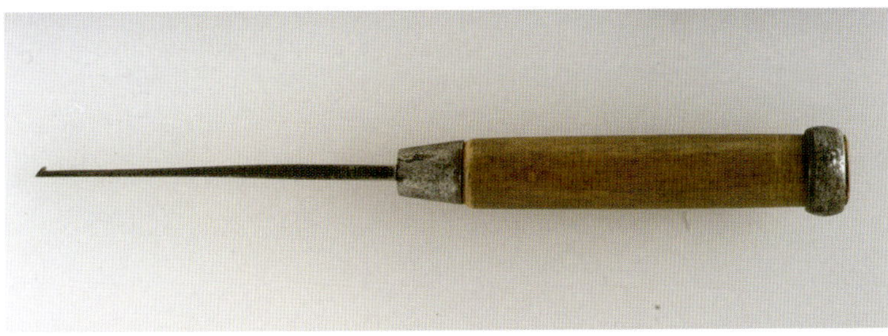

This chisel is also used to correct a hole in a hole to stop digging, which is not penetrated. At the bottom of a hole to stop digging, there is always a mountain-shaped hole left. The harpoon-shaped blade tip is driven into the hole and pulled up to break it down. This chisel is named after the shape of its cutting edge.

SICKLE CHISEL

This chisel is also used for adjusting the hole to stop digging. The angle where the bottom of the hole and the side of the hole meet is precisely adjusted. This type of chisel is a thrusting chisel. The cutting edge is a double-edged small blade. There are two types of cutting edges, one is a double-edged knife and the other is a harpoon. They are used for small work such as fittings.

◎Photos courtesy of Takenaka Carpentry Tools Museum

CHISEL SETUP

Chisels Require Setup, Including Adjusting the Kan (Ferrule) to Avoid Damaging the Handle

Like planes, chisels also require a setup process before use. This setup involves adjusting the kan (ferrule), but with various methods available, it can be confusing. Here, Noboru Tsuchida explains an easy-to-follow method suitable for beginners.

No Need for Wood Compression on the Handle: The Tsuchida Method for Kan Adjustment

The chisel setup involves two main steps: sharpening the blade and adjusting the kan. While sharpening is covered on page 126, this section focuses on the kan adjustment.

The process of adjusting the kan is also known as kan-awase. Typically, chisels are sold with the kan loosely fitted halfway onto the handle. The purpose of the kan is to prevent the handle from splitting, so it should ideally be positioned 2–3 mm below the top of the handle. This adjustment is referred to as kan-sage (lowering the ferrule).

Without lowering the kan, the hammer (genno) will not strike the top of the handle directly, reducing the force transferred to the blade. The kan is not lowered during production because the handle may shrink due to drying, causing the kan to loosen.

Various methods for adjusting the kan are shared in books and on social media. Here, we introduce the method recommended by Mr. Noboru Tsuchida, who appeared on page 92.

A kan with a slightly larger inner diameter than the one included with the chisel.

A metal file and pliers.

A block of wood for securing the chisel during the process.

Start by removing the kan. While rotating the handle, tap the handle shaft with the genno. This should allow you to easily remove the kan.

Check the difference in the inner diameters of the kan. The narrower side will be inserted onto the handle. Note that this orientation is likely the opposite of the temporary fitting at the time of purchase.

Firmly grip the kan with pliers and file down the inner edge of the narrower side to create a chamfer.

The chamfer should be about 0.5 mm wide. After filing it a bit, place the kan over the handle and then check the fit. Stop chamfering once you can push it about halfway onto the handle by hand.

Next, secure the chisel in the block of wood, place the kan onto the handle, and position the slightly larger kan over it. Tap with the genno until the kan is 2–3 mm below the top of the handle.

When removing the chisel from the block, be cautious. Forcing it out by moving it back and forth can damage the blade.

Mr. Tsuchida recommends using a vice to secure the chisel whenever possible to prevent damage.

A widely used method involves compressing the handle (wood killing) by striking it with the genno to reduce its diameter, making it easier to insert the kan.

However, Mr. Tsuchida advises against this, as it disrupts the wood fibers.

Additionally, some people recommend hammering the top of the handle after lowering the kan to flatten and expand it over the kan.

Check both sides of the kan for differences in inner diameter and confirm which side is narrower. The wider side should face the top of the handle.

Firmly grip the kan with pliers and file down the narrower inner edge with a metal file to create a chamfer.

Place the kan onto the handle, position the slightly larger kan over it, and tap it down. The process is complete when the kan is positioned 2–3 mm below the top of the handle.

Though flattening the handle top after lowering the kan is often recommended, Noboru Tsuchida asserts that it's completely unnecessary.

To remove the temporarily fitted kan, lightly tap along the shaft of the handle from the blade side with a genno.

When the kan is removed from the handle, note that the orientation will be reversed after lowering it.

Mr. Tsuchida disagrees with this approach, stating that it reduces the impact force by creating a cushion effect. Once the kan is lowered, no further modification to the handle top is necessary.

There are also methods where the curved end of a crowbar is placed on the kan and struck with a genno, or where the kan is directly hammered into place. Both can damage the handle and kan, and Mr. Tsuchida advises against them.

CHISELING TIPS

Digging Aggressively All at Once Is a No-Go: Take Your Time and Carve Steadily and Carefully

If you can process joints and mortises, then you're well along on your woodworking way. However, in the world of carpenters, there's a saying: "Five years to master boring holes." There's no need to rush—just refine your skills step by step. Here, we provide the very basics of mortise digging.

Be Careful Not to Get Injured—Chisels Are Sharp Tools

Let's start with some key points for handling a chisel.

Hold the upper part of the handle with your non-dominant hand. Apply some grip strength, but keep your elbow relaxed.

On the other hand, keep the elbow of the hand holding the hammer (genno) relatively high. If the elbow drops, the hammer won't strike the top of the chisel properly and may hit the hand holding the chisel.

Use the flat side of the hammer's head, and ensure that when the hammer strikes the chisel's handle, their centerlines align perfectly. Always keep this in mind.

Use a chisel narrower than the short side of the mortise. Narrower chisels tend to penetrate better, and many people use chisels around 0.6 inches/15 mm (gobu) or 0.9 inches/24 mm (hachi-bu).

Among hand tools, chisels are the most prone to causing injuries. Always ensure that no part of your body is in the path of the blade. Changing your stance frequently while digging is also important for safety.

If you force a dull chisel, it may slip and cause an unexpected accident. Always handle chisels with the utmost care.

When you're ready to start digging, secure the practice wood firmly with clamps. Chiseling under unstable conditions is a recipe for accidents.

Use a carpenter's square to ensure right angles and mark the surface of the wood with ink lines.

For marking, it's best to use a fine-point water-based pen for clear lines. Avoid oil-based pens, as they tend to smudge.

Each Dig Should Be About 0.1 Inch/3 mm—Haste Makes Waste

The first step in mortise digging is marking the area with ink lines. Surround the area you'll carve with these lines. The precision of this step determines the success or failure of the mortise, but remember, this is just practice. Even so, use a carpenter's square to draw precise lines.

The next step is making shallow cuts with the chisel, called nori-dachi. Place the flat back of the chisel facing outward and make shallow cuts around the inside edge of the ink lines to prevent the wood from tearing.

Now it's time for the main digging. Position the chisel about 0.1 inch/3 mm inside the ink line, with the back blade facing outward, and strike it vertically. However, don't try to dig too deep at once—0.1 inch/3 mm is sufficient. If you attempt to carve too deeply in one go, the blade may wobble, leading to mistakes.

After creating the initial cuts, insert the chisel at an angle with the back facing upward and carve toward the center of the marked area. Again, avoid digging too deeply in one go.

Return to the same spot and strike vertically, then repeat the angled cuts. Perform the same cutting process from the opposite direction as well, gradually deepening the hole.

Occasionally, strike vertically about 0.1 inch/3 mm inside the ink line along the long side to deepen the cut.

When you reach the desired depth, align the chisel along the ink line and make vertical cuts to finish shaping the mortise.

The key is to maintain a consistent vertical angle when striking the chisel. If the angle deviates from vertical, you won't achieve a clean mortise. Take your time and carve steadily and methodically to improve your skills.

Before starting the main digging process, place the chisel's edge just inside the ink line and lightly tap it to create shallow guide cuts.

Next, position the back blade of the chisel about 0.1 inch/3 mm inside the ink line and strike vertically. It's important to keep the chisel perpendicular to the surface.

Tilt the chisel slightly and carve inward to scoop out the material. Return to vertical strikes, repeating this process.

For finer carving, you may need to push the chisel with both hands. Be careful not to let your hands slip.

The task of increasing the flatness of the back blade through the process of uraoshi (flattening the back). The chisel is being sharpened with vertical strokes.

GRINDING AND SHARPENING

The Life of a Chisel Lies in the Flatness of Its Back Blade, Which Must Be Maintained in the Best Possible Condition Through Proper Sharpening

For chisels, the genno is a crucial partner, but the whetstone is equally important. If you neglect sharpening, the tool will lose its functionality. Ultimately, the effectiveness of a chisel is determined by how well it is sharpened. To enhance its cutting power, mastering the sharpening process is essential.

Has the Chisel Already Been Sharpened? Do You Need to Prepare It?

The process of preparing a chisel for use after purchase is known as shitate. In some cases, this involves not only lowering the collar but also sharpening the blade.

However, determining whether or not a chisel needs sharpening during shitate can be challenging. This is because of the following background:

In the past, hand-forged chisels were shipped without being fully sharpened. This was because the sharpening preferences varied among carpenters, who were the primary customers, and the manufacturers would stop partway to accommodate these preferences. However, as DIY activities have become more popular and beginners have increased, there has been a growing demand for chisels to be ready to use, changing the situation.

Even today, some chisels are still sold without being fully sharpened, but most are now sold in a polished state, meaning they can be used immediately after purchase. That said, it's not always clear whether the sharpening has been done to perfection or if it has only been partially completed. Even if it has been sharpened, it is unclear to what extent the process has been carried out.

This variation makes it difficult for retailers to provide accurate information, and it is almost impossible for beginners to make a judgment. As a result, it is generally safer to sharpen the chisel as a precaution during shitate. That is the most prudent approach.

Incidentally, the sharpening process during shitate is essentially the same as regular sharpening. Please proceed with the steps outlined for regular sharpening below.

Sharpening with a swinging motion (naname-togi or diagonal sharpening) is easier to hold than vertical sharpening.

Achieving Flatness in the Back Blade Is the Core Theme of Chisel Sharpening

The back blade of a chisel consists of a continuous flat surface, except for the shallow hollowed-out area known as the ura-suki. In woodworking, the flatness of this surface is extremely important because the back blade acts as a guide when cutting. Any distortion will prevent proper insertion and lead to inaccuracies in the cuts.

The process of sharpening the back blade to enhance its flatness is called uraoshi, and chisel sharpening begins with this step.

First, prepare a medium-grit whetstone around #1000. Press the front blade with your fingers and place the entire back blade on the whetstone, moving it back and forth to sharpen.

During this process, to avoid reducing the ura-suki, slightly lift the handle. However, this adjustment requires precise control. If lifted too much, the entire back blade will not contact the whetstone. The key is to let the area near the neck lightly touch the whetstone.

Positioning the chisel perpendicular to the long edge of the whetstone is called horizontal sharpening (yoko-togi), while moving it along the long edge from a short-edge direction is known as vertical sharpening (tate-togi). While horizontal sharpening is common for uraoshi, Nakajima from Kosho Hitachi prefers vertical sharpening to avoid horizontal scratch marks on the back blade. However, this technique requires skill, so he advises beginners to start with horizontal sharpening. After a certain amount of sharpening, shine a light on the back blade to check for distortions. If the surface is flat and smooth, the uraoshi with the medium whetstone is complete.

Next is the sharpening of the front blade, which has a beveled edge. For the front blade, vertical sharpening is fundamental. However, naname-togi (sharpening with a diagonal swinging motion of the chisel axis) is also easier for beginners due to its stability, though it tends to slightly round the blade edge. While sharpening, ensure that the entire beveled surface of the front blade is consistently in contact with the whetstone. The bevel angle, which defines the cutting angle, is typically set around 30 degrees. If this angle changes during sharpening, it can lead to a loss of sharpness or make the blade more prone to chipping.

Applying force with your fingers near the blade edge makes it easier for the entire bevel to contact the whetstone. When the blade edge begins to form a burr (ha-gaeri), it's time to switch to a finishing whetstone.

MAINTENANCE AND STORAGE

A Sharpened Tool Lasts a Lifetime with Proper Care

Chisels, with their sharp cutting edges, require careful handling not only during use but also in storage. Leaving them unattended on a workbench is out of the question. Additionally, since chisels are prone to rust, preventive measures should be taken.

Protect the Blade with a Homemade Cardboard Sleeve

Maintaining chisels is relatively simple. After use, clean the blade and handle, and apply oil to prevent rust. Compared to planes, chisels require less attention.

A sleeve for chisels made by cutting cardboard and wrapping it with tape—it's almost free to make!

Covering the chisel with this sleeve prevents the blade from colliding with other chisels and protects it in case it's accidentally dropped.

There is some debate in the industry about the type of oil to use—whether plant-based or mineral-based is better. In practice, either works, and there's no need to overthink it. Inexpensive mineral-based sewing machine oil should suffice.

As precision tools, chisels demand careful handling. Craftsman Hitachi, who contributed to this guide, always uses a cardboard sleeve when the chisels are not in use. This method protects the blade from damage and enhances safety. It's easy to make, so consider adopting this approach. Tips for Handling and Storing Chisels.

When setting down a chisel during work, place it on its bevel face down to protect the delicate edge. For storage, use a canvas chisel roll with individual pockets for each tool. These are convenient for transport and can be purchased for as little as 1,000 yen.
Preventing Rust

As chisels are made of steel, they are prone to rust. If you're not using them for an extended period, consider wrapping the blade in plastic wrap for protection. With proper maintenance and storage, a chisel can become a lifelong companion.

No need to be particular about oil types—affordable mineral oil is sufficient

OTHER JAPANESE WOODWORKING TOOLS

The world of woodworking is filled with a wide variety of tools, each fulfilling its specific role. These range from essentials for DIY projects to tools that go slightly beyond the typical home hobbyist's scope. This chapter introduces some of these tools, helping you rediscover the fascination of traditional woodworking hand tools.

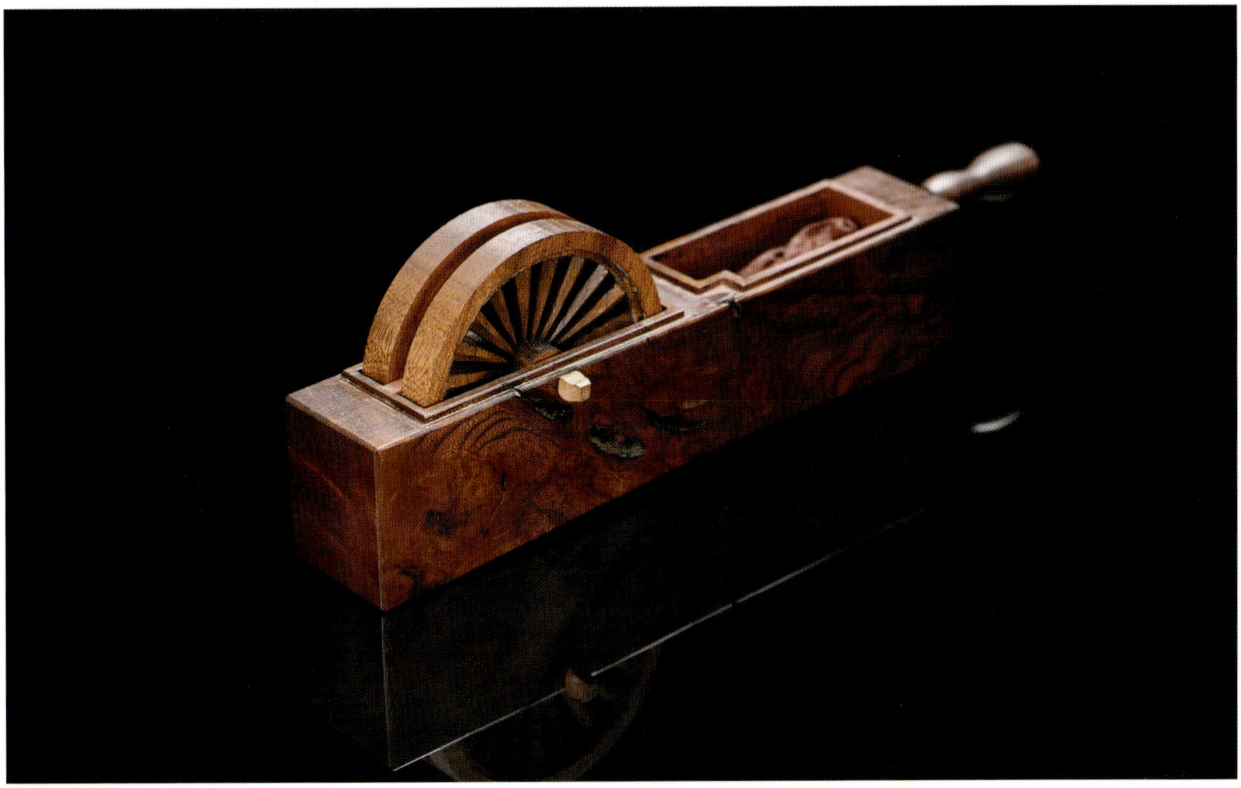

Whetstones from the basic to ones sharpening with #1000, #4000 and #10000.

GRINDSTONES: AN INTRODUCTION AND GRINDING TIPS

Enhancing Precision with the Three-step Sharpening Process That Enhances Blade Sharpness

The three-step sharpening process using whetstones determines the sharpness of a blade, enhancing precision. Like plane blades and chisels, whetstones demand careful attention because the sharpening method can drastically alter a blade's cutting ability. This guide introduces beginners to the intricate world of whetstones.

The Era of Synthetic Whetstones and Their Grit Numbers

Visit any home improvement store, and you'll find a vast array of whetstones, enough to overwhelm any shopper. The packages display numbers preceded by #, which indicate the grit size. Higher numbers mean a finer surface texture.

While grit size is mostly standardized across brands, slight variations in hardness and blade adhesion create subtle differences, leading to personal preferences. Choosing your ideal whetstone can be challenging, especially for beginners. It's best to start with reputable brands and decide after gaining some sharpening experience.

Today, synthetic whetstones dominate the market. Natural finishing stones were traditionally used for the final sharpening step, but advancements in synthetic technology have made them the preferred choice for even the finest work. Natural stones, once essential, are now rare and expensive, often costing several times more than synthetic options. High-end natural stones can range from tens of thousands to over a million yen.

While natural stones have unique qualities, such as preventing over-polishing, they have become luxury items, often out of reach for DIY enthusiasts.

Diamond whetstones for surface flattening.

Recommended Whetstones for Beginners: Medium and Finishing Stones

Sharpening involves three steps: coarse, medium, and finishing. While grit size is mostly standardized across brands, slight variations in hardness and blade adhesion create subtle differences, leading to personal preferences. Choosing your ideal whetstone can be challenging, especially for beginners. It's best to start with reputable brands and decide after gaining some sharpening experience.

Coarse Whetstones: Used for major corrections, such as repairing chips or reshaping the blade angle. These whetstones have coarse grit sizes and high cutting power.

Medium Whetstones: The backbone of the sharpening process, crucial for restoring a blade's sharpness. With advances in synthetic whetstones, tasks previously requiring coarse stones can now be handled with medium ones. These are also used for leveling the blade's backside (back-beveling).

Finishing Whetstones: Used to remove fine scratches from medium sharpening, smooth the blade, and enhance sharpness. For ultimate precision, ultra-finishing stones (#10,000 and above) may be used, but they are unnecessary for most DIY tasks.

Typical Grit Ranges:

Coarse: #100–#300

Medium: #800–#1200

Finishing: #5000 and above

In addition to sharpening stones for each stage, flatness-maintaining diamond stones (around #150 grit) are also essential. Beginners are advised to start with:

Medium stone: #1000

Finishing stone: #6000

Diamond stone: #150–#180 for surface maintenance. These three tools are sufficient for DIY purposes. Japanese synthetic whetstones, renowned for their world-class quality, will help you unlock the full potential of hand-forged blades and chisels.

Move the blade back and forth while maintaining the cutting angle.

SHARPENING GUIDANCE

Hand Tool Sharpening Brings Out Superior Performance Over Electric Cutting

The wood surface planed with a hand plane is far more refined than those achieved with electric tools. Chisels can also perform precision work that rivals electric tools. To fully unleash the power of hand-forged tools, your sharpening skills must be, uh, well-honed.

Constantly Flatten the Whetstone to Maintain a Flat Sharpening Surface

The method for sharpening chisels is covered on page 126, so here we will focus on sharpening planes and summarize key points. There are various opinions about sharpening techniques. The method introduced here is just one way of sharpening. Whetstones should be placed on a stone holder during sharpening, but the holder itself is not very expensive. Placing a wet towel under the holder can stabilize it, so give it a try.

Before using the whetstone, it must be soaked in water. However, the soaking time varies depending on the type and manufacturer of the whetstone, and soaking it for too long can weaken its strength. Be sure to read and follow the instructions provided with the whetstone.

The first step in sharpening is flattening the surface of the whetstone. The sharpening surface of the stone becomes uneven as it is worn down by the blade, particularly in the center. Sharpening on an uneven surface will result in an uneven blade edge, making proper planing impossible.

Flattening the sharpening surface of the whetstone is typically done by rubbing it with a diamond stone.

For beginners, it may be difficult to judge whether the surface is truly flat. A recommended method is to draw a grid pattern on the surface of the whetstone with a soft pencil and rub the surface with a diamond stone until the pencil marks disappear. With practice, you'll be able to judge by the feel of the diamond stone whether the surface is flat.

The frequency of flattening is also important. While the pressure applied to the blade can vary, those seeking precise planing should consider flattening the surface after about ten strokes. Use the pencil grid method to find your optimal frequency. Don't neglect the flattening process.

When flattening the surface, don't forget to round the corners of the whetstone's surface with the diamond stone to avoid injuring your hands during sharpening.

If the surface of the whetstone is uneven, the blade cannot be properly sharpened. Frequently use a diamond stone to flatten the surface.

Ensure the Ito-Ura (Backside) Is Flat Through Proper Back Beveling

Sharpening a plane blade begins with back beveling, similar to chisels, to ensure that the backside and the edge are flat.

In the past, when plane blades were shipped in an unfinished state, back beveling was a tedious process requiring extensive grinding with a metal plate and abrasive grit.

However, with the general availability of "90% finished" or "ready-to-use" planes, back beveling has become much easier. The same applies to chisels. Back beveling is done with a medium-grit whetstone around #1000.

Using an oil-based marker, color the "ito-ura" area to distinguish between the sharpened and unsharpened parts.

As mentioned earlier, vertical sharpening is ideal. However, beginners might find it easier to position the plane blade perpendicular to the long edge of the whetstone and use horizontal sharpening.

A key tip for all sharpening tasks is to avoid long strokes, as changes in applied pressure can occur. Beginners should keep their strokes relatively short.

Add water occasionally and use the entire surface of the whetstone during sharpening.

When sharpening, do not press the entire backside of the blade onto the whetstone. Instead, slightly lift the head side. Pressing the entire backside will reduce the back clearance. Applying pressure toward the cutting edge naturally positions the blade for optimal sharpening.

When the cutting edge and the ito-ura become a continuous flat surface, you're close to finishing the back beveling.

If some areas remain dull and are difficult to sharpen, they may still be marked with the ink from the marker.

In some cases, extensive grinding is necessary, requiring the process of ura-dashi (backside raising).

Ura-dashi involves lightly tapping the bevel with a hammer to push that area outward on the backside. This delicate process should be done carefully.

While some recommend ura-dashi for chisels, planes and chisels have different structures. It's best for beginners to avoid this technique.

Finish by polishing both the front and back with a finishing whetstone. Shine a light on the backside to confirm a flat, distortion-free surface before concluding the back beveling process.

Understanding the characteristics of each whetstone will lead to great results.

Sharpening Brings Life to Tools: Regularly Remove Burrs

Some people prefer to only sharpen the front side to avoid losing the back clearance. However, hand tools deform with use. If you don't sharpen to correct these deformations, the cutting edge won't be restored. For a sharp cutting edge, start with back beveling and then move on to sharpening the front side.

Before sharpening, inspect the cutting edge. If there are major chips, they need to be corrected with a coarse diamond stone.

If there are no chips and the back beveling is complete, begin sharpening the front side with a medium-grit whetstone around #1000.

Ensure the bevel is fully in contact with the whetstone and maintain a consistent angle while sharpening.

Professional sharpeners recommend vertical sharpening rather than horizontal. If the plane blade doesn't fully fit the whetstone, diagonal sharpening is acceptable.

However, vertical sharpening can be challenging for beginners, as the cutting edge may roll back and forth, leading to a rounded bevel. Fix your wrist and move the blade back and forth using only your elbow to prevent rolling.

Diagonal sharpening provides stability but can result in a skewed cutting edge. Alternating pressure on the left and right sides can help address this issue.

As you sharpen with the medium whetstone, you'll notice black slurry forming and a slight burr appearing on the backside.

Burr formation is a sign of sharpening progress, but it's important to remove it before it grows too large. Large burrs can damage the polished cutting edge. Regularly flip the blade and remove the burr.

Once the steel cutting edge becomes a glossy flat surface, move on to a fine whetstone around #6000 for finishing.

Finishing whetstones are soft, so avoid applying excessive pressure. While you may add water occasionally with medium whetstones, rely solely on the slurry for finishing.

Alternate between sharpening the front and back sides during the finishing process. Once you can no longer feel the burr by touching the edge, the finishing process is complete.

Compared to intermediate sharpening, finishing takes less time.

It's curious how simply sharpening against a whetstone brings a sense of calm to the mind.

GRINDSTONE HISTORY

Natural Whetstones from Kyoto Began Production in the Early Kamakura Period 800 Years Ago

Natural whetstones mined in Kyoto are known domestically and internationally as being of the highest quality, attracting global buyers in recent years. Their history dates back over 800 years.

A Finishing Whetstone Coveted by Enthusiasts, Reigning at the Pinnacle of the Whetstone World

With the advancement of synthetic whetstones, the mainstay of rough and medium whetstones shifted from natural to synthetic early on.

However, in the case of finishing whetstones, natural ones—particularly those from Kyoto—maintained a superior performance and continued to reign at the top of the hierarchy.

Products like Nakayama and Okudono were treated as luxury brands and commanded high prices.

The tide began to shift about 20 years ago. The performance of synthetic finishing whetstones improved dramatically, gradually encroaching on the position once held by natural whetstones. Today, synthetic whetstones have become the standard for finishing as well.

Even among professional carpenters, more and more have never handled natural whetstones. The transition was driven by performance and price differences. Natural whetstones could not compete with the affordable synthetic alternatives.

Nevertheless, there are still those who continue to use natural whetstones from Kyoto for finishing, claiming they offer a sharpness that only natural stones can achieve.

This reputation appears to have taken root overseas as well. The large number of foreigners purchasing natural finishing whetstones in Kyoto is evidence of this.

Additionally, no other nation values sharpening tools as much as Japan. The reason for foreign buyers may also lie in their desire to experience the essence of Japanese culture.

So, how did Kyoto's natural whetstones, which dominated the market, come into existence? The raw material is sedimentary rock, formed from oceanic plankton called radiolarians with hard shells and fine particles of sand that settled on the seafloor over time.

Carpenters have prized this rock for its hardness, ideal for sharpening blades.

This rock was formed near the equator of the Pacific Ocean about 250 million years ago. It was carried by oceanic plates and eventually created a vein of natural whetstones around Mount Atago, northwest of Kyoto, spanning about 30 kilometers east to west. This was a grand geological event.

The sharp, angular shells of radiolarians embedded in the rock made it exceptionally suitable for sharpening blades.

While sedimentary rock layers exist throughout Japan, the unique combination of ideal hardness and accessibility in a major city gave Kyoto a distinct advantage in producing finishing whetstones.

Valuable whetstones on display at the Takenaka Carpentry Tools Museum.
◎ Photography cooperation: Takenaka Carpentry Tools Museum

The Retired Emperor Gotoba Praised Kyoto Whetstones, the Most Expensive Item Among Carpentry Tools

Kyoto whetstones rose to fame around 800 years ago, in the early Kamakura period.

Honma Touzaemon Tokinari, who governed the Umekohata area (now Ukyo Ward, Kyoto City), presented whetstones mined from his territory to Retired Emperor Gotoba.

The emperor, known for crafting swords himself, was highly impressed and praised Tokinari, calling the whetstone "excellent."

Possibly under orders from the emperor, Minamoto no Yoritomo, who had just established the Kamakura shogunate in 1190, appointed Tokinari as the chief overseer of whetstone mining in Kyoto, encouraging production.

From then on, the Honma family oversaw mining operations, spreading the reputation of Kyoto whetstones throughout Japan.

Incidentally, Kyoto's finishing whetstones are called "Honzan Awasedo." "Honzan" is short for "the Honma family's mountain," while "Awasedo" refers to the combined use of blade and whetstone, meaning a finishing whetstone. Thus, Honzan Awasedo translates to "finishing whetstone mined from the Honma family's mountain."

However, a trademark dispute in the mid-Showa era led to a change. What was once a name exclusively for whetstones from Umekohata, governed by the Honma family, was broadened to refer to all finishing whetstones mined in the Kyoto area.

Honzan Awasedo is still regarded as the highest quality today, with patterns resembling clouds or crows on the whetstone surface becoming objects of admiration, emphasizing its aesthetic appeal.

Today, it's not uncommon for Honzan Awasedo stones to cost tens of thousands of yen, and exceptionally rare premium stones can fetch hundreds of thousands or even millions of yen. It's no wonder natural whetstones are considered the most expensive carpentry tool. The price surge is attributed to resource depletion, a growing concern for enthusiasts and professionals alike.

ADDITIONAL TOOLS

Acquiring These Tools Will Undoubtedly Expand Your Skills and Ability

Home projects can't be performed and completed necessarily with just a plane, saw, hammer and chisel. It's the support tools that allow you to bring your creations to life. Some tools are essential for basic tasks, while others help you achieve a higher level of craftsmanship. Here are a few selected tools.

The Type of Tools You Use Will Greatly Vary Depending on What Kind of DIY Project You Aim to Undertake

Even within DIY, there is a wide variety of interests. Some people want to make chairs, tables, or shelves, while others dream of renovating their homes or even building a log cabin. Recently, there has been an increase in enthusiasts who focus on planing wood into thin shavings, dedicating themselves to perfecting this art.

These individuals aim to participate in competitions such as the kezuroukai, which are held nationwide to showcase thin shaving techniques. In a broad sense, this too can be considered DIY, and by using relatively expensive hand-forged planes, they contribute to the growth of the industry.

As an aside, some in the industry wonder if similar events could be organized for hand-forged chisels and saws.

With such diversity in DIY, not only do the types of planes, chisels, and saws differ, but the supporting tools also vary significantly.

For instance, a sumitsubo (inkpot) for drawing long ink lines is generally unnecessary for typical DIY projects—usually, a square ruler will suffice. However, if you plan to renovate or build a log cabin, it becomes an essential item.

DIY projects can change direction midway, and discovering new tools might open your eyes to new woodworking fields. Keeping a keen eye out for interesting tools will lead to a more fulfilling DIY life.

That said, DIY is not a cheap hobby. For beginners starting from scratch, it's recommended to first purchase a square ruler (sashigane), clamps, a straight edge, a rail base (repurposed from old rails) for adjusting plane blades, sharpening stones, a metal tape measure and a bar-shaped metal file. Further purchases can be balanced with your budget.

The following introduces tools frequently used by craftsman Hitachi, excluding clamps. If commercial products don't meet their standards, they make their own. Some of the tools mentioned here are custom-made.

SQUARES

Essential for accurate right angles, a precision ruler made to JIS standards

For marking lines, a square ruler (sashigane) is often used for right angles. However, the accuracy of a sashigane is not very high. In situations requiring precise 90-degree angles, a sukoya is used. Made according to JIS standards, it offers exceptional accuracy. Prices start in the 1,000-yen range, making it relatively affordable for a professional-grade tool.

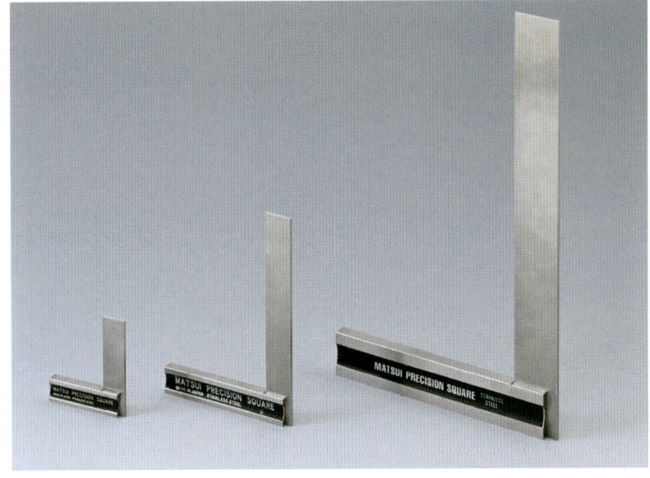

Various sizes are available and can be purchased at hardware stores.

BOTTOM EDGE RULERS

For checking the flatness of a plane's bottom edge, enabling precise adjustments

This wooden ruler is an invaluable tool for checking the distortion of a plane's bottom edge. Many products feature a notch to avoid contact with the blade. In the past, it was common to make your own, and the one in the photo is a custom-made piece by craftsman Hitachi. Commercial products range from the affordable to the high end. In addition to wooden ones, stainless-steel straight edges are also available.

A custom-made bottom edge ruler by craftsman Hitachi, with a wooden handle attached to a metal blade.

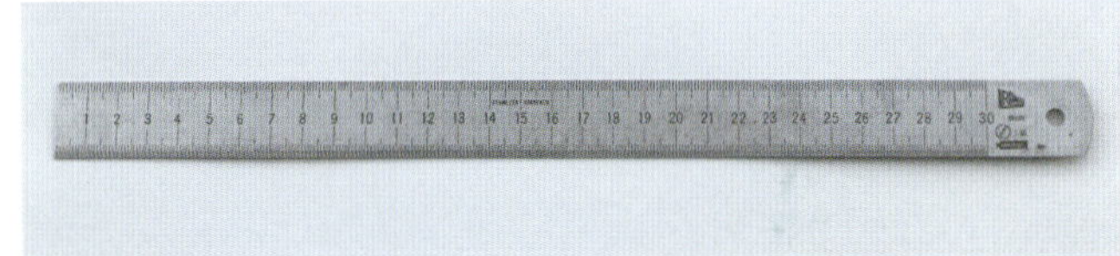

Straight edges also come in a wide range of price points.

FREEDOM HAMMERS

A ruler that allows for any angle, useful for marking non-right-angle joints

Also known as an angled ruler, it features a mechanism where the long and short arms are secured with a screw, allowing free angle adjustments. It is used for marking lines for non-right-angle joints like dovetail joints and is a powerful tool for making complex joints. A similar tool with a built-in protractor is the protractor, which provides precise angle measurements.

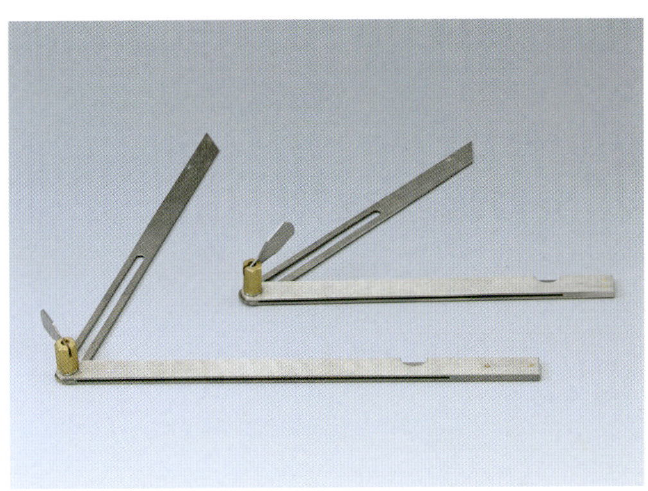

The angle can be freely adjusted, making it useful for drawing non-right-angle lines.

SUMI INK BOTTLES

Essential for drawing long ink lines, especially for large-scale projects

The ink-soaked thread is pulled taut, lifted slightly, and then released to create a long, accurate ink line. While unnecessary for DIY projects that can be completed with a simple square ruler, it becomes essential when working with larger materials. The reel at the back is used to wind up the thread. For professionals, making their own sumitsubo is a given, and they often compete in craftsmanship. However, inexpensive versions are available at DIY stores.

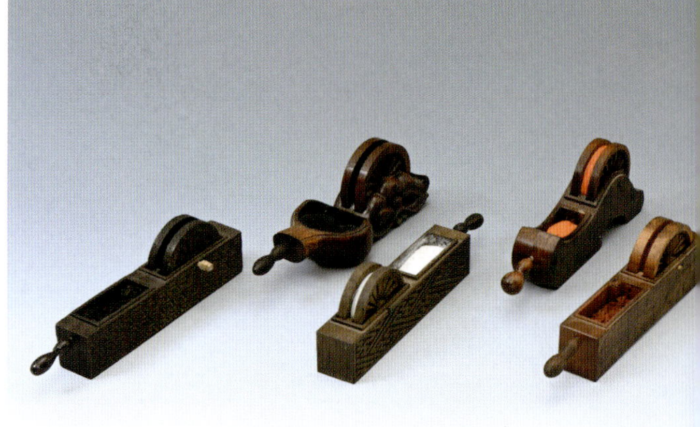

A handmade sumitsubo (inkpot) by craftsman Hitachi, with a quality worthy of being called a work of art.

ANVILS

Necessary for adjusting the back of a plane blade—no need for expensive ones

Also written as tetsu-doko (iron anvil), it is commonly used as a workbench in metalworking, though it has limited use in woodworking. However, it is indispensable for adjusting the back of a plane blade. A lightweight, relatively inexpensive anvil will suffice. The photo shows three types: the rail base on the right, the honeycomb base with holes in the center, and on the left, a custom-made anvil by Hitachi crafted from soft lead to prevent damage to the plane blade during adjustment.

The rail-type base on the right in the photo is relatively affordable and easy to find.

INSERTION TOOLS

An L-shaped right-angle ruler, a must-have for DIY projects

Used for measuring length and right angles, as well as for marking lines. The longer side is called nagate (long edge), and the shorter side is called tsumate (short edge). Some versions display both metric and traditional Japanese units (shaku and sun). There are also advanced types that can measure the circumference of a log when its diameter is measured or that display diagonal lengths. The sashigane is surprisingly deep in functionality, and its price is often more reasonable than expected.

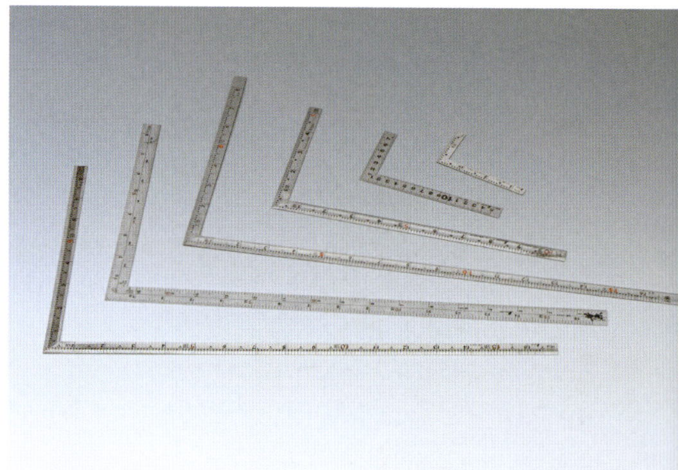

Various types are available on the market, depending on their length and features.

Drawing ink lines with a prized umitsubo produces a beautiful, straight line.

CLAMPS

Essential from the start of DIY to ensure accurate work

A tool that firmly secures materials to the workbench. It is indispensable in DIY, not only for improving precision but also for preventing accidents. The most common types are C-clamps and F-clamps. F-clamps are better suited for securing thicker materials. They're a low-priced essential, so it's a good idea to buy several in different sizes.

Select the best size according to the material's thickness and width.

RULED LINES

Enables accurate parallel lines for marking without a ruler

It consists of a guide plate and a movable rod. By sliding the guide plate along the reference surface of the material, the blade attached to the rod marks a line parallel to the reference surface. It is easier and more accurate than drawing lines with a ruler. Once used, it becomes indispensable. There are also types with two blades, useful for marking mortise holes and for marking the same width on multiple materials.

The right side shows a type with two blades, and the left shows a type with one blade.

SMALL KNIVES

A handy tool for everything from chamfering to cutting material

A small knife is invaluable for fine chamfering or cutting small sections of material. There are two main types: kiridashi kogatana (cutting knife) and kuri kogatana (curving knife). The kiridashi kogatana has a wide blade, while the kuri kogatana features a sharp blade that extends to the base of the handle. Due to the growing number of collectors, well-known products are now traded at high prices.

A custom-made small knife by Koshō Hitachi with intricate designs and a sheath, similar to Hakone craftwork.

OSA RULERS

A ruler made of numerous bamboo skewers for copying curved surfaces

This specialized ruler is used to trace the shape of a curved surface, such as the curve of a log. It captures even the surface's irregularities and is essential for advanced construction like sukiya-zukuri (traditional Japanese tea houses). While not commonly used in general DIY, it is good to be aware of such tools if you plan to take on large-scale projects. The photo shows a custom piece by Koshō Hitachi, made with over 500 bamboo skewers.

The left shows the state before tracing, and the right shows the state after tracing the curve.

KAGAKI GAUGES

A modern high-tech version of the marking gauge, with added caliper functionality

It has the shape of two overlapping stainless steel T-shaped rulers. This relatively new tool can accurately mark parallel lines along the reference surface of the material, just like a traditional marking gauge. Additionally, it can function as a caliper, allowing the T-shaped ruler to slide for precise measurement of material thickness and groove width. It is relatively expensive, priced in the 10,000-yen range, a digit higher than traditional marking gauges.

One T-shaped ruler is hooked onto the reference surface of the material for marking.

JIGS

A device that secures tools and materials, contributing to efficient work

This group of implements includes items like anti-slip devices for workbenches, various custom rulers and more. While jigs are essentially meant to be self-made, the process begins with thinking about how to work safely and efficiently. Designing and creating jigs is also one of the joys of home carpentry and woodworking.

A variety of wooden rulers custom-made by Koshō Hitachi to improve their efficiency.

Books to Span the East and West

Tuttle Publishing was founded in 1832 in the small New England town of Rutland, Vermont [USA]. Our core values remain as strong today as they were then—to publish best-in-class books which bring people together one page at a time. In 1948, we established a publishing outpost in Japan—and Tuttle is now a leader in publishing English-language books about the arts, languages and cultures of Asia. The world has become a much smaller place today and Asia's economic and cultural influence has grown. Yet the need for meaningful dialogue and information about this diverse region has never been greater. Over the past seven decades, Tuttle has published thousands of books on subjects ranging from martial arts and paper crafts to language learning and literature—and our talented authors, illustrators, designers and photographers have won many prestigious awards. We welcome you to explore the wealth of information available on Asia at **www.tuttlepublishing.com.**

Published by Tuttle Publishing, an imprint of
Periplus Editions (HK) Ltd.

www.tuttlepublishing.com

ISBN: 978-4-8053-1964-2

Daiku Dogu no Kihon Tsukaikata kara Maintenance made
Mokko Tedogu no Chishiki to Gijutsu ga Minitsuku

Acknowledgments

※ Kosho Tsuneari Co., Ltd. assisted in photographing the planes, saws, gennos, chisels and other tools in each chapter of the book. Also, Masao Nakajima, president and master carpenter of the company, and Haruhito Sasahara, a staff member of the company, provided technical advice and appeared as operating models.

Distributed by:
North America, Latin America & Europe
Tuttle Publishing
364 Innovation Drive
North Clarendon
VT 05759-9436 U.S.A.
Tel: (802) 773-8930
Fax: (802) 773-6993
info@tuttlepublishing.com
www.tuttlepublishing.com

Japan
Tuttle Publishing
Yaekari Building 3rd Floor
5-4-12 Osaki Shinagawa-ku
Tokyo 141 0032
Tel: (81) 3 5437-0171
Fax: (81) 3 5437-0755
sales@tuttle.co.jp
www.tuttle.co.jp

Asia Pacific
Berkeley Books Pte. Ltd.
3 Kallang Sector, #04-01
Singapore 349278
Tel: (65) 6741-2178
Fax: (65) 6741-2179
inquiries@periplus.com.sg
www.tuttlepublishing.com

Printed in China 2505EP
28 27 26 25 10 9 8 7 6 5 4 3 2 1